The Power of Love Energy

Shauna Hibbitts

DEDICATION

This book is dedicated to the purest form of love that I've ever had. To have the most gracious pleasure of experiencing the highest love exchange between my late husband and I. The late Lorenzo R. Hibbitts. I will always love you internally and eternally.

Thank you to my advanced readers and all dear believers in the *Power of Love Energy: Positive Love* is something that we all deserve to have and exchange with that special someone. Start with loving yourself first. Do what it takes to form habits that will allow you to grow personally, and to invite more and more positive vibrations and love within yourself.

To my dear widows and widowers, you hold a special place in my heart.

Note to all: When love finds you hold onto it for dear life. Grow with love, nurture it, be kind to it, absorb it in your mind, body, and soul. Once mastered, it is one of the best kept secrets to having constant fulfillment and happiness in your life.

Gracias Con Mucho Amor,
Shauna Hibbitts

Testimony by Nicole Albach, Shauna's Childhood Friend and Sister

Lorenzo and Shauna were the true definition of love that definitely withstood the test of time. They accepted each other for who they were. Including their flaws, bad habits, fears, insecurities and challenges all while providing for each other's needs. They displayed their love that was full of encouragement, trust, loyalty, honesty, openness, help, and most of all love.

Table of Contents

(Lorenzo Hibbitts approved Chapters 1-5)

Chapter 1

WE MET

My husband and I met at a family backyard BBQ party that happened every summer and was so much fun to attend. If you let my husband tell you, he spotted me there the summer before. He mentioned that I didn't pay attention to him. He also said he fell in love with me at first sight. We didn't share that same sentiment and it would often surprise him when I told him I did not believe in love at first sight.

Truth is, I was freshly out of a relationship with my child's father and was finding myself again. This relationship was 7 years long and it was toxic. I was new at winging this as a single parent and knew I had to be cautious with my choice of men moving forward. Now there were two of us to consider and I placed that very highly as a parent. At the time, it was not viewed highly to raise your child by yourself. The thing is, I knew deep down my life was supposed to be on a different path and in order for me to see that, I had to move on and not worry about the world's standards.

While not being concerned with the world's standards, I was in college, working full-time, and being a mom all by myself when I met Lorenzo. He was a single dad, separated from his first wife, and was completing his college degree as well. In the second year, I had fresh eyes and saw him right away at the party. He was handsome, funny, witty, and full of life. I was ready to start living again and worked hard to get myself in a good mind space to do so, while still being a work in progress.

We both loved to play the card game spades and we both shared a very competitive spirit yet fun nature about ourselves. Lorenzo was also grieving and this was something I did not know or understand at the time. I didn't recognize what grief looked or felt like. It was not until years later that I understood his grief during the entire time of our relationship. Lorenzo lost his mother a year before we met and she was only 39 years old.

Lorenzo's love and connection with his mother was very extraordinary. He was her only child and they were extremely close. He spoke very highly of her. I know this through stories Lorenzo shared with me and from his family. Witnessing a person losing a parent is difficult. He said a day did not go by that she was not in his thoughts. Whenever he spoke about her transition and funeral, he was a totally different person. I would just listen and hug him.

It was unreal because of how perfect we were for each other. We both could not believe that we were from the same town and had not met each other until the party. I was 23 years old with a five-year-old son and Lorenzo was 23 as well. I am 5 months older than Renz (as I affectionately called him) and I often would joke in our relationship and remind him I was the oldest. We had so much humor and laughter from the start. I knew that the world interpretation of this exciting love is what's known as the butterfly stages yet, I could not help but believe that this was not true. At least for me, I soulfully believed in true pure love.

Back to the card game; which was very intense, focused, and extremely fun. The four of us could not get enough of joking around and we played game after game. He played with his Uncle Eric and I was paired up with my good friend and sister, Nicole. You better believe we whooped them so badddddd…I mean badddddd! Now, according to my husband's recollection, the whooping was on us…hmm, I don't think so! Lorenzo was what they called a trash talker on the table yet so polite. Trash talking was feeding your ego and tearing down your opponent's game plan; all in fun. I never trash-talked on the table. I was a quiet player and would surprise you with my moves. He took me all out of my character as we would go back and forth trash talking and we were both magnetically engaged with one another as if we were the only two playing.

As the party was winding down into the night, I saw Lorenzo escorting a young woman to her car. I don't know what came over me but I touched his arm so he would pause and I asked him if he was leaving. This was not my style but I could not get enough of being around this guy. He told me he would be right back. I asked him if that was his girl. He told me no, and that she asked him to walk her to her car. He added, "I don't even know her and I don't have a lady". He always used the word lady to describe females and I just fell for that. My whole insides were screaming, "I'm a lady I know how to love and treat myself". Of course I kept myself super cool. After all, I was wearing an airbrush t-shirt that said "All Men Were Dogs," a common rap song at the time and how I felt in the aftermath of my break-up. To my surprise, Lorenzo thought the shirt was humorous and didn't match my personality. Again, I was finding myself in a process.

Is this guy a gentleman as well? I thought they were extinct? I often told my Granddad Ledger they broke the mold after him because I never saw such a doting father and husband with gentlemen qualities outside of him. He called my Grandmother "Queen" and set an incredibly high bar on how to treat and respect a lady. Lorenzo had these qualities as well and my grandparents adored him. When Lorenzo returned from escorting the young lady to her car, we exchanged numbers and serious all-nighters on the phone for months. If you know me I don't care much for the phone, never have. I had so many butterflies in my stomach I couldn't get enough of chatting with him. We spoke about everything from our upbringing, what we believed in and our educational and future goals.

Honestly, he was the first guy I ever spoke to about deep meaningful stuff with and he was all in. Lorenzo was a super handsome, intelligent young man that always had a plan and knew where he was going. It was like a needle in the haystack to see someone just as driven as me and I was fiercely attracted to it. He was like a drug. I could not get enough of him and knew I needed to spend more time with him, yet at a slow pace. I was only away from a long-term relationship for a year and I had a 5-year-old son.

Testimony by Cynthia Pardon, Shauna's Best Friend & Sister

What I admired most about their relationship was the fact that they never compromised their love. Never let anyone or anything negatively penetrate their happiness and love for one another. They kept the outside noise out which is very hard to do in this world and society.

Chapter 2

THE ROMANCE BEGINS

As I mentioned before, I had a 5-year-old son and thought, how do I do this? Do I include Terence right away around him? Should I just get to know this guy myself first? I prayed and meditated daily and have been since I was a child. I was raised in the church and understood the power of taking God everywhere I ventured in life. I believed in trusting my instincts so I did. I dated Lorenzo for 6 months before he met my son personally and I abstained from sexual activities.

It was important to me to get to the core of his heart as a man then to let sexual encounters blur the scene. Secondly, he was technically a married man although separated and living on his own. I was not getting mixed up in all of that. I needed to see divorce papers before I engaged myself physically with him. We both also took an AIDS test to make sure we were clean and shared our results with each other. I saw something so special between us that I did not want anything to spoil it. He was a gentleman and was very supportive of my feelings. He got the divorce paperwork signed, sealed and delivered. The divorce was granted, the AIDS tests were negative, and we were ready to keep venturing on.

We began building a friendship and grew closer each day. It may not have hurt that I also told him he could date and have his lady friends while I got to know him. To this day, he could not believe I was open to that and he never experienced that before with a woman. I had faith we would be a great couple if we took our time and heck we were only 24 years old. He also had a black book (that is an address book with lady friend names in it) and he had stars next to each lady. I used to laugh at him about his rating system years later. I never made the book. He said I was above the book. Thank goodness!

I was mature enough to know this was a very handsome, smart guy. So I refused to put that type of pressure on him. I also knew the mystery of a sexual encounter would make it more fun and he would desire me more above any other lady that he befriended. Have my husband tell you, he says it was a smart trap that I placed him in. We both laughed about it and I always told him that I really needed that time to make sure he was the one. I knew he was a responsible individual and if it was meant for us things will work out for our future.

Our first date was at Cedar Point Amusement Park that was located in Sandusky, Ohio. Oh, what a beautiful day it was. It was warm, full of sunshine, and just the two of us. I'm what you call a bag lady. I tend to carry items that I may or may not need and Lorenzo wasn't used to that. When we got there, I narrowed down a few of my belongings in a backpack. He kept trying to get me to leave it in the car, yet I couldn't. I wore glasses, contacts, and needed my hair to look good all day so I carried a comb, brush, and of course a headscarf. My experience at Cedar Point has mostly been sun-shining days, but there was always a chance of rain. So I carried a change of clothes and thought I would add a dry men's t-shirt to the mix. I love wearing men's t-shirts, so this was nothing for me to have a few on hand.

When we were near the Blue Streak roller coaster Lorenzo took my hand and held it as we walked. I must admit this was the first time a young man ever held my hand. He caressed my hand, which at first felt very weird to me. The whole time I kept thinking what he was thinking about. I told myself to roll with it and it was a very sweet gesture. I definitely felt like a lucky lady because we didn't see couples holding hands that often.

Out of the blue clear sky, a thunderstorm appeared and we ran to the nearest shelter and restroom area. Did I mention I also carried folded windbreakers in my purse? Well I had one for each of us and of course two dry shirts. He was so happy and appreciative to get into a dry shirt and have a windbreaker for the drizzle that came shortly after. I of course did the slick back low pony hairstyle to stay presentable and hopefully pretty for him. We closed Cedar Point down. We were one of the first cars there and one of the last cars leaving. He never questioned me carrying a bag again whenever we went on adventures and gave me the nickname "Bag Lady".

After that date, Lorenzo wanted to pick me up from work any time he could. He was in school and worked at the airport. He would take the bus and the train at times, but he loved having a car. I was finishing my first degree, being mommy, and working part time at the arena downtown formerly called The Gund Arena. This is where the Cleveland Cavs games, special events, and concerts were held. I traveled throughout the city on the bus with my child to attend everything from school to events and work. I could get off at midnight sometimes and was alone traveling on public transportation. So I was happy whenever Lorenzo wanted to pick me up.

The Power of Love Energy

I managed several concession stands that worked well with my school schedule. The first time he came to pick me up, I got out around midnight. I waited outside the arena for him. We spoke about a pickup time the day before via landline phones. We didn't have cellphones and had to trust one another. Time went by and I didn't see Lorenzo. I always had a bus pass because that was my life at that time. I waited and waited. It was almost 1am and I kept thinking this guy was not the type to stand me up. Something must have happened to him. We've been on dates spoken on the phone for hours and months. I just didn't think he would bail out of our courtship this way and he would tell me if he didn't want to be with me anymore.

He pulled up at about 1am. He was very nervous and excited. I was still there waiting for him. He got into a fender bender and had to wait for the police to file a report. Back then you were supposed to wait for the police to arrive. He asked me, "What made me wait?" I told him I knew he was coming and that something must have happened. That I felt like it wasn't his character to stand me up. He said he was so surprised I waited for him and he was happy to see me. Today if anyone asked, he would tell them he knew then that I would always have his back and that sealed the deal for him as far as my loyalty. That felt good every time he said that even after all these years.

I then was ready to introduce my son to him in our sixth month of dating. My son loved his father and had a hard time understanding a new person in his mom's life. It was an adjustment for all of us and one thing I can say about Renz is he had the ability to put himself in someone else's shoes. He never pressured my son into anything. He let my son be and do what felt natural to him in the relationship between them and among the three of us. I loved

16

Lorenzo for so many things, but to accept my child and me with his whole heart ranked at the top for me.

The next several years we spent almost every moment together. The black book was tossed out and hopefully burnt. Those 3 years were incredible. We went to the movies, ate out, and listened to music all day long. We had daily calls and we even started spending the night at each other's houses. So many long walks and bike rides together. Going to the park was especially delightful as we spoke about everything in detail from childhood to our early 20's. At the same time, we were both working on our college degrees and motivating and supporting each other. In addition, we surround ourselves with like-minded, beautiful, positive couples. And then this happened...I turned 30! Ayyyy yaiiii yaiiii!

Ladies and gentlemen please don't get twisted for your 30th. You could really hurt yourself. That's exactly what I did...I got twisted.

Testimony by Sul Pillow, Shauna's Nephew

My Titi and Tio had a beautiful relationship filled with love, happiness, and respect. I feel blessed just to be able to have witnessed it first hand. Although all relationships are different, they definitely set the standards for me for what marriage should be. They are one of my favorite couples and I will forever love them.

Chapter 3

THE BREAKUP

As my 30th birthday was approaching, Lorenzo and I had the most wonderful few years together. Then, I started having "The Talk" with Lorenzo. You know the one that starts like, "So we've been together for a while and I was wondering where do you see our future heading to?" Yes, I was caught up in that 30-year-old trap, the one in which you tell yourself you need a huge life change.

Almost like check-marking your life span of events or you will die kind of thing. It seems like today this has not changed and is happening with young men and women. I'm here to tell you to watch the trap you may be setting up for yourself. Have goals, be ambitious, take small steps, pray, and meditate on what you truly want. Life has a way of socking it to you fast and furious. Certain situations you place yourself in will make your own head spin.

I added the marriage pressure at the age 30 on Lorenzo. After a while, it wore on him. I had become obsessed with this. Not to mention my lack of maturity in handling a young man who had an early failed marriage under his belt. He was still recovering from the scars of that relationship.

We both had a heart to heart talk. Lorenzo felt like he wasn't ready for marriage and I felt like I was. We both were very sad with the mutual decision to break up. We both knew we didn't want to ruin our friendship, along with keeping the positive memories in place. Therefore, we broke up for one year. There were no arguments, just no more discussions on the marriage topic. I got all in my feelings as sometimes a young woman does. We stopped talking and seeing each other. Neither one of us could tell anyone why we were not together when folks asked about it and couldn't say an ill word against each other either. We went our separate ways for a whole year.

I was so lost that I started going back to church for answers. I met someone there who wanted to marry me. My desperation to be married and check it off my list was so high that I slipped hard without knowing and I said yes. I married a complete stranger, I didn't know who I was anymore, and got lost in the man-made religion.

I say it like that because my strong connection with God from birth was compromised with rituals and out of the norm behavior for church goers such as, heavy judgment for one another, and questioning one's faith or relationship with God. I was in a situation that depleted myself, my finances and my life was topsy turvy. I was a stranger to myself. I was walking around speaking only in terms you learn in church and could not have a straight human conversation. I felt like a robot. It was awful and writing this now reminds me of how you must stay true to yourself.

I was so angry with myself and was married to someone I didn't even like. My friends and family were highly concerned about me and for good reason. What I couldn't say to them was "I knew I fucked up" yet, they couldn't do anything for me. I had to get myself out of this, and fast! I am a private person and this was so public...ugly public. OUCH.

This whole marriage fiasco was totally my fault. We were not supposed to be together at all. He was highly religious and never contributed to the relationship. He was a taker. He questioned every move I made and even despised me if I was alone with my family. He had to be in the know at all times. He was pretty insecure and paranoid. I hit rock bottom and had to figure out how to get out of this mess. Keep in mind my son is older and watching me. He was so resilient...Thank God. He went with the flow and stayed close to me. My son always believed in me and felt like I always had the answers. He looked up to me and still does to this day.

This marriage did not last long, but felt like an eternity to me. I managed to separate myself from the stranger I married and get some time to myself to figure out how to break this off. This was very challenging because I was with someone that was heavily into church and professed his love for me. In other words, he did not want to end the marriage.

Remember, earlier when I said I thought I was ready for marriage and later I discovered I was not? Yep, this is where I learned that hard lesson. How the hell did I get myself into this? Talking about asking for something you are not prepared for at all. The most important thing is there is a stuck feeling when you do get married...the question is, are you stuck with the one you should be with? I clearly was not. I had to find myself again and start building back up everything from my spirit, confidence, and my bank account.

The Power of Love Energy

Keep in mind, I still had a little guy and prayed I didn't ruin him with this. Meanwhile, Lorenzo and I never crossed paths in our small city in over a year. We often joked about those years as time went on and thought how could that even happen? Like that's crazy we never saw each other. We both knew it wasn't meant for us to see each other.

When I dusted myself off and sought clarity in my life, I came back stronger. I did my research and found out I could dissolve this marriage as long as we both agreed and it was within 6 months. I had to convince the man I married that we needed to end the marriage. He did not want to end it. I thought OMG what am I going to do...I cannot! At this point, we were living separately, and I moved in with my sister. He had a hard time allowing me to do this, but I had no choice. I had to tell this man that we could start over, go slow, and get to know one another. Then we can remarry the right way. Such a lie, but again I had no choice. This is what I had to do to get my life back on track.

I felt like I owed Lorenzo an apology for the unannounced break up, and then for me meeting and moving on to some crazy random act of self-destruction that had absolutely nothing to do with him. This was all because I needed to have a check on my list based on age expectations I applied on myself. I encourage anyone reading this please do not restrict yourself with a checklist. Age is truly just a number, as the late Aaliyah coined beautifully in a song. Keep striving for what you want in life and take it slow.

So, you know what I did next? I called Lorenzo. Talk about feeling embarrassed, lost, and found. Yet, my conscience would not allow me to move on with my life without closure with him. He had female company. I was not surprised this handsome, intelligent gentleman I let out in the wild was not supposed to be alone. I always loved how open we were in our communication. I apologized for the reasons above. You know what he said?????? "I would like to see you, I missed you." I was thinking, "Huh, what are you really serious?" I did not expect that and I planned on going on with my life with a clear conscience that I did the right thing by clearing the air between us. We really enjoyed each other and I never had a time like that in my life and I thought I may never experience that again.

Meanwhile, I am still in the middle of getting my affairs in order to dissolve this untimely, crazy situation I got myself into. Lorenzo offered to help me get out of this and would joke that he knew I lost my mind and made a mistake. He found the dissolution of the marriage template for me and guided me on answering the questions and submitting the forms. I was so in love with this man and never stopped loving him. I felt so bad about how everything went down. When the dissolution was over, I thanked Lorenzo and thought we would go our separate ways. I was wrong. He joked and said you got a mistake behind you and so do I. Speaking about us both having a previous marriage. Then he went on to say, "Now let's stop playing and live the life we both want to live together."

Testimony by Sabrina Ledger, Shauna's Sister

Lorenzo and Shauna's marriage was built on trust and love. I admired their soulmate relationship. Some people never come across their soulmate, but my sister and brother-in-law found one another. It was a relationship I witnessed to be genuine and real just like a love song. Music that lives on in Shauna's heart forever.

Chapter 4

REUNITED

We spoke for months about this breakup and shared what we both learned about ourselves in the process. All of a sudden, we were so consumed with our new life together that we ended up never speaking about any of this anymore in our lifetime. Forgiveness is a powerful thing. Lorenzo was the first person that ever showed me how powerful it really is and how it releases you more than anything.

We both at that moment decided to choose each other and go slow. We continued our relationship for the next three years. We had regular date nights, family nights, and supported each other with our work projects, dreams, and aspirations. We both admitted to each other that we admired each other's drive and desire a better lifestyle. We both believed if we worked hard, we could have the life of our dreams.

Lorenzo and Terence's relationship grew stronger each day. I took a step back and let it come together naturally. Having a blended family is tricky and the last thing I wanted to do was make it harder than it needed to be. I surrendered to the process of our relationship. When I did that, guess what happened next?

Lorenzo proposed to me! WOW, WOW, WOW!!! Unexpected and right on time at the same time. I encouraged a 2-year engagement but Lorenzo was ready to get married after one year. My engagement year was a great one! We moved in with each other and got to know each other on a new level. This was our first time living together.

I had two major experiences under my belt that got me clear on the importance of taking a relationship you want so badly in slower steps. I was not going to lose Lorenzo again because he wanted things to go at a faster pace. I had already seen what happens when you rush a relationship. So we both agreed that was best especially if you believe you want to spend the rest of your life together. The purpose of this is to allow you both space to grow.

As time went on, our bond grew stronger. We both knew in our hearts what the natural next steps were and we were ecstatic to take them together. We got married in Las Vegas and planned to book the "Say I Do Drive Thru". Yep, I know what you're thinking. There is a stigma that Vegas weddings don't last and let alone in a drive thru. LOL! We thought it was a super hilarious, unique way to do this and we were both all in for the fun. I am here to tell you that as long as you have each other and genuinely put your relationship first, it does not matter where you get married.

OMG, I was so nervous that I accidentally ripped a small area of my beautiful dress that my Aunt Pat made for me! I was supposed to be walking out of the door to the limo that we all chauffeured in. Instead of walking to the limo, we had to make calls for help instead. We called the hotel staff for a sewing kit and luckily got that taken care of right away.

Meanwhile, I am about 20 min late, no cell phone and hoping Renz knew I was coming. When we got outside, which was a beautiful day in Vegas, he let out a sign of relief when he saw me. He whispered to me that he thought I changed my mind. I whispered back to him you are crazy and I told him what happened at the last minute.

That day we talked about for years and made it a habit every anniversary to look at our photos and reminisce together. We also created time to speak about our feelings about that year and about our love. We were totally open about what we loved within the past year. Self-improvement as individuals was a personal goal of ours and we spoke about how we wanted to excel as people. Eventually, these chats became very frequent, at least weekly professing what we loved about being with each other. Over the years, I wanted to be a better listener and share that with my husband. Lorenzo took the lead in this area for me and he was an exceptional listener. He coached me through the stages of better listening. I am a work in progress and still working on this skill to this day.

One year he wanted to work better by communicating with me about finances. There was a time early in our relationship where he would bottle up and keep anything he saw on the horizon that could affect our plans negatively to himself. When I caught on, you guessed it, it was when I could not help and it was too late.

We spoke about this and realized transparency is key. I shared with him that I know back in the day that men carried so much on their backs, but this is a different day. I told him I am unable to help you if you don't let me in. I mentioned how I could help with some problem solving techniques, which is what he was already doing for me. Renz had to get used to the idea of receiving this exchange in return. He caught on quickly and from then on, we held weekly financial meetings to see where our budget was and how to manage it together.

This was a huge revelation for the both of us. That we can depend, rely, trust, and embrace each other for anything that came our way. This is exactly what we did and it was a beautiful thing. I cannot tell you how fascinating it is to be yourself with someone that doesn't judge you but wants to see you succeed as a person. Nothing like it.

As time went on, we spent every moment together. Outside of work and school, when you saw Renz you saw Shauna. We were inseparable and knew the power of LOVE we had for one another would stand the test of time. Life has a way of throwing some serious curve balls and we believed in our marriage. Protecting it was numero uno.

We both matured and understood no one would have our backs like we would for each other. We both buckled down and finished school, picked up certificates along the way, and got involved with real estate and managing our own businesses. We worked together as a husband and wife dynamic duo. We were partners.

One of the things that I asked my husband was if there was anything I did that hurt his feelings or bothered him, to please come to me to speak about it. I agreed to do the same. We knew that couples did not stay together long if their communication was off and we didn't want to be a statistic.

I got so crazy about this love I asked Lorenzo that we never use the D-word in any conversation we have with each other or others. I believed that if you bring certain words and energy to your marriage it could take it down the wrong path. What we had was too special and there was no need to sabotage it. The world already couldn't wrap their minds around our love and there were forces or energies that tried to get in the middle. We reminded ourselves daily that we were brought together for a reason.

Testimony by Tanita Wiggins, Shauna's Childhood Friend and Sister

The love story of Lorenzo and Shauna is the true definition of Black love. I witnessed how a man should treat a woman, how a husband should value his wife, and how a Queen honors her King. The Hibbitts love story is an inspiration for us all.

30

Chapter 5, PART A

WE DISCOVERED THE SECRET OF BUILDING A STRONG FOUNDATION

W e continued as a team to support, love, and cheer one another. We both agreed that one of the biggest takeaways of our love and relationship is self-improvement. Self-improvement is an individual journey and at the same time, you need to check in with each other for accountability. You need to cheer each other on while you are learning and growing in your journey. Everybody has a love language in their relationship. Lorenzo and I were very passionate about many things and one of our passions was our love. We were both on the same page about the importance of how to continue to nurture and grow our relationship on a daily basis.

Saying "I do", and getting married is just a ceremony. Showing the world that this is the person that I choose to be with me for the rest of my life is a commitment. Marriage is much more than a ceremony and it goes beyond the exchange of rings. One would think that marriage has to do with what the other person can do for you, yet in reality it is all about what you can do for yourself and contribute to the team. When I say for yourself, I do not mean in a selfish way I mean in a way that gets you growing in the direction that you need to bring your best self to the relationship. That means digging deep and finding areas in your life that may need to be fleshed out. You want to be prepared to address things that may come up and could sabotage the marriage.

We all have a history before getting married and have lived through an early childhood. There may be some forgiveness that we need to do for ourselves and for others. Above all, we need to give ourselves a lot of grace and time. Stay consistent and learn to have fun throughout it all. There will be some frustrating times and there are many things that happen in life that affect a marriage. The best thing that I can tell you is that Lorenzo and I prided ourselves on how we responded to life. Our motto was there are only solutions, no problems. Anytime I ran into a jam, I would run to him and say, "I don't know what to do!" My natural reaction was to get hype when life hit. This was a behavior that was modeled to me growing up and I had to learn how to solve problems in my best mindset.

I had to process and learn that not everything has to be solved on that day. Lorenzo showed me how to do this by first being an example in his life and on his journey. He was the best model teacher for this and allowed me to go through this without criticism. The importance of being honest to yourself and articulating your feelings will strengthen your communication in your relationship. Kindness, love, and treating each other like gifts took our relationship to another level.

Looking through both our lenses helped us when we had to make decisions together during challenging times. The delivery of our messages to each other was just as important as what needed to be spoken about. We both consciously communicated with each other through love. We listened to each other and gave each other space to process the challenges that were happening. At the same time, we continued doing nothing but be loving and kind towards each other. We never let a challenge get in between us.

These are just some examples of what we did in our relationship:

- The secret to having a successful marriage lies within you. You are the reason why a marriage can be so successful. NOTE: *both parties need to want this*.

They need to be on the same page when it comes to the importance of marriage and the relationship.

Here are the ingredients for a great marriage and fulfilling relationship:

- Marriage is what you make it and fulfillment and happiness is achievable on a daily basis as long as both parties want these attributes in their relationship.

- Everything is achievable with communication, love, honor, truth, respect, compassion, and admiration for one another. These are also principles we need to hold in high regard for ourselves and allow positive reflections in the marriage.

- Be careful with who you have around your marriage. Lorenzo and I accomplished a lot in our relationship personally and as husband and wife. If you meet anyone that is very close to our relationship, they will tell you we were very private people and carried ourselves with a high degree of discretion that protected and shielded our love against the world's standards.

The Power of Love Energy

We lived by the principles above and this does not mean that we were not outgoing or did not party from time to time. We had a very full life and enjoyed every minute. The difference was what happened in the marriage stayed between us and we did not go outside of ourselves to seek outside counsel or to share our deepest darkest secrets with the world.

We both agreed from the beginning that was one of the mistakes many marriages make – sharing everything with the world. When conversations occur outside of the marriage, this in turn stops the nurturing in the marriage, which can lead to a breakup. It was important to us that we were private when it came to the details of our marriage. Having a public life and a life that is private is perfectly fine and allows you the freedom to live and continue building upon a strong foundation. You can still engage with others and you want to make sure that who you are engaging with are positive people that believe in marriage. Being around people who support your love for each other and people that are cheerleading your continued growth as a couple is important.

I received wise counsel when I first got married from a married woman and close friend. She's still married to this day. She told me when I got married that it was still good to have friends that happened to be single. They need to be friends that respect marriage and have similar foundations and philosophies as their beliefs. Same for married couples. I have to be frank here, all married couples are not created equal. Therefore, be wise in your selection of married couples as well and find the right fit when you're spending time with others.

Here are a few secrets that lead to a healthy positive marriage:

- **_Listen_** to one another. There is not a time I recall Lorenzo not listening to me. He was my sounding board and told me the truth. He had no shame in telling me what I was doing right or wrong. I was able to receive this because I knew it was always coming from a place of love and he had such a polite way of delivering his thoughts. When I did not want to hear about what I was doing wrong about a problem, I would politely tell him you are very handsome but I'm not hearing this right now. I need time to process and I'll get back to you. Then I would say I would try to work on that; especially if I knew deep down I was getting in my own way.

- **_Honesty_** is key and if you are not honest with yourself, you cannot be honest with your partner. Human nature does not allow it to work that way. We all know someone that has tried to live a double life and how far that goes in life. If you're looking for a pure, fulfilled life, this area must be addressed. Establishing honesty from the start of the relationship is crucial. Until you do, the other steps will not matter. Our time is our most precious commodity. No matter how driven we were, nothing else mattered.

- **_Being present_** is a massive task at times. We have to practice this. It's a top priority to nurture and continue to feed your relationship daily. Even if it's a quick coffee in the morning together or chat before you leave the bedroom. So many small pockets of ways to check in on one another. Always check to see how your spouse is doing and feeling.

- ***Communication*** according to the *Webster Dictionary*, communication is a process by which information is exchanged between individuals through a common system of symbols, signs or behavior.

My husband would always express to me all the time that communication is the _result_ of what was communicated. For example, the result should match what you desired the outcome to be. If the communication is off, then the style that you communicated needs to change. If you want your partner to help more around the house, be up front and ask for what you need. Whenever Lorenzo and I did not see eye to eye on a subject, we agreed to disagree. The process does not have to be a shouting match. We both politely would look at each other and say, "We will keep working on this, or I'm not feeling this right now, or I'm having trouble understanding." I had to keep practicing and make sure I was present with the conversation at hand.

- ***Compromise*** along with strong communication is easier said than done. As long as you work on a regular basis keeping the communication clear, you will be able to achieve this goal. One of the biggest compromises Renz and I had to make took about a year to accomplish. We were able to joke about it years later and called it our "TV Story". We had a TV in our bedroom and I noticed Lorenzo needed to watch TV to de-stress after work. The TV would be on all day and when it was time for our nighttime routine, it was still on. Now, we both read and write, and I love reading before bed in silence. It was difficult for me to do so with the TV on. I was a flight attendant and I also worked at a hotel at the time so when I was home I wanted a little more peace from working with the public.

There is a back-story here. Lorenzo was heavy into finance and real estate with the mindset of creating multiple streams of income. He was currently the property manager of the building we lived in and had his own management company on the side with his business partner. He was also part of a Masonic Family in Cleveland, Ohio Excelsior #11. This organization celebrates the teachings of Freemasonry, charity, brother and sisterhood, and self-improvement to obtain outstanding characteristics. He became a Past Master (the title given to the Master of the lodge after they served their leadership time for the lodge). He often said it was the best brotherhood and sisterhood that he ever was involved in. He absolutely loved the order along with all of his brothers and sisters.

The television was his escape from everything and how he kept up with current events. It was an added form of education for him. He was always learning and trying to make sense of the world and how he could contribute to it.

There was only one problem, I could not read or sleep with the television on! I asked him if he would turn the television off at a certain time because my mind wandered and the light bothers my eyes. I wear glasses and corrective contact lenses and my eyes became very sensitive to light. He could not understand why it bothered me so much, and I could not understand why he needed it every night.

I let months go by not sleeping well and going to work cranky. When I say cranky, not cranky to others but to my inner self and wishing I had a better night's rest. I came back months later to talk to him about it. What I've learned about being with a man is that you have to pick the right time to have certain conversations. The beauty of knowing this will also help with the communication process. I was not a complainer and never wanted to be that type of woman with anyone period. I never liked that when I experienced that from others. I also did not want to be the "go with flow" kind of girl either. I always questioned my inner self about how something made me feel.

After several months, I revisited the conversation again and asked him if we could move the TV in another room. I suggested that after he finished watching TV in another room, he could come into the bedroom and complete his nighttime routine. At the time, we did not have a TV in the living/dining room. It surprised him that this still bothered me and he said he had a gift for me and he will give it to me the following week. He said the gift would solve this problem and all would be well.

I was excited about the gift and for this problem being resolved for the last and final time. The next week he had my gift on my nightstand. Do you know what my gift was? Earbuds and a facemask to block out the sound and the light from the TV. I am laughing as I am writing this.

Yes, it is funny now but you had better believe it was not funny back then. He saw the look in my eyes and he knew I was not feeling that at all. Whenever I was quiet, he saw the look on my face, and he would joke and say, "What Shauna? I'm trying to solve the problem." The problem with being married to a romantic, handsome man that loves you is that it can be extremely difficult and challenging to get mad at him.

He was really trying to work with me on this TV situation. It just was not the answer for me. I struggled for a few months scratching and shaking my head with the earbuds and facemask on. We were both working hard to compromise on this. More time went by and I just could not reach the level of deep sleep I needed. I could not take it anymore so I decided after my nighttime routine I would sleep in the living room until he fell asleep. Then I'll turn the TV off and go to bed. One night he got into his shows and noticed I was gone. He came into the living room and was like "Shauna what are you doing?" I told him that I will come into the room when he is done watching TV. This got his attention and we were about a year in working on a compromise that worked for both of us. He was like, "No way are you sleeping in another room. I'll move the TV out of the room tomorrow."

We hugged and kissed and I was thrilled that the day had finally come. My husband had always been a man of his word and I loved him for that. He took the TV out and watched it in the living room and came into the room when he was ready for bed. We both recognized easily how many other things we could enjoy in the bedroom without a TV. The TV stayed out of the room for just a year.

We eventually upgraded to a fancier TV that had a timer set on the remote. We also had more time to talk about the "TV story" and learned a lot about ourselves in the process. I noticed that Lorenzo used the television as a transition to go to sleep and I used reading or listening to music. The TV always kept me awake. So, we brought the TV back to the room with this new feature. He would let me know what time it was scheduled to shut off and I worked on my transitionary activities lining them up closely to that time. Lorenzo got his transition and I got my deep sleep back. Boom! It took a year to solve, but we were both determined to figure out a way. This was hard and took a ton of patience from both of us, process, and growth. We made it happen and we were both proud of ourselves. We are all different people and to expect to agree on every single thing is unnatural and not healthy. I loved my husband so much he was my friend, mentor, coach, lover, and number one supporter. All of his plans included the best for our future.

Lorenzo always had my full attention and I took his advice like it was gold. Especially, because he took his own advice first and it showed clearly in his life. There were times where I didn't agree. It could be on current affairs, or the way we should handle a problem, or something new he wanted to do like investing heavily in the stock market. I would say, "No, I don't agree with that and I don't think the time is right." You could imagine how Renz looked because he was so used to me saying things like, yes all the time, you're right, or I agree with you. And he would say, "Shauna why not?" I would tell him because this took years to get on the same playing field for both of us. I would say, "What about our emergency fund or savings?" Which is what he taught me about and took years to get me onboard and work those avenues. He used to shake his head when the student gave him back his lesson plans.

Lorenzo and I were brought up with traditional systems yet we also had modern twists in our relationship. Basically, whoever is available and can take care of x,y,z, did the work. Cooking and cleaning is another form of love with your partner and showing how much you care about your life together. For us, this system worked. We both shared what we liked and disliked the most about housework. You would be surprised what your partner doesn't mind doing if you just have the conversation. We worked together as a team to get the job done no matter what we worked on or had to make decisions on. We believed it was a team effort.

Testimony by Mercedes Battle, Shauna's Niece

Tio was a phenomenal man. He loved my Titi and would have done anything for her. He took her nieces and nephews in as his own. He offered guidance, words of wisdom, the strength that everyone needed. A protector and always made sure he was an important factor in my Titi's life. How he protected her, helped to protect us.

Chapter 5, PART B

WE DISCOVERED THE SECRET OF BUILDING A STRONG FOUNDATION Continues...

To reach the key to a man's heart, one must take note of his characteristics and what makes him tick. This process is so important to grasp. Especially, if you are a very independent, strong, opinionated, and high spirited person such as I am.

All of the characteristics that my husband has, along with my characteristics, were exactly the magnetic attraction we had for one another from the start. This knowledge helped support and foster the relationship.

I'm all about women's liberation, fairness, equality, and all of the things that help bridge the gap between us and men in the world. Yet, the truth is men and women are unique in their makeup and thought processes. As a woman, I had to understand this and know when in my relationship to be the assertive queen that I am and when to allow my king to be the man. My king could only be as great for our kingdom as long as I knew when to let him be the king in certain spaces of our relationship. He has to know you have his back especially in public and that we know when to step back and let him rule.

My husband became Worshipful Master for his Masonic Lodge in 2014. He did an amazing job for his lodge and his love was never unnoticed by his brothers and sisters. I accompanied on many events before, during, and after his role as the Worshipful Master. I had my own brand, was self-employed, a board member for an organization, a mom, and held other titles. In this arena, I was his wife, life partner and number one supporter. He was in charge and it was my duty to support that. This is just an example of how you may need to silently support your husband in public and in different spaces through life. You are merely doing your job as a wife and understanding your role changes based on certain factors. A man loves a woman that doesn't get twisted on that. That clearly recognizes when certain things need to go the way they do to reach certain goals together. Lorenzo always told me he was the luckiest man in the world to live the life he was living with me because I got what was real and what mattered.

Our kings can only be great if the queen works her magic in all aspects of the relationship. At the same time, a man needs his man cave and a woman needs her she shed. Yes, we believed in that and both made sure we carved out space wherever we lived to have this. We both knew how important it was for both of us to have this alone time and experience that consistently within our relationship.

Here is our list of do's/don'ts that up-levels a positive relationship:

- ***Don't go to bed angry***. This is something both of us always agreed on from the start. Try to have your issues settled to a point where you don't carry an attitude to bed. Your marital bed is so sacred and deserves the best version of yourselves as a unit. Try to keep the peace here. Drink some tea or watch a show to calm down any anger or anxiety lingering before bed.

- *__Say "I love you often".__* Of course you could show love in many ways. There is nothing like taking the time from your heart and expressing these simple but powerful words. Both Lorenzo and I felt we could conquer the world when we expressed this to each other.

- *__Surprise each other.__* One of my favorite things to do. We both enjoyed surprising one another with simple things. I used to write notes and add it to his lunch when I packed it or buy him a small gift for any day: no holiday needed for me to do this. He would come home early when I thought it would be a late evening. I absolutely loved that he worked so hard. I can't tell you how many times I found small gifts from him. He would do things as simple as getting my favorite candy bar, Reese's Cups.

- *__Plan dumb shit days together.__* I created dumb shit days (DSD) because at some points of our relationship we were both driven entrepreneurs who needed to slow it down. These days were scheduled in our shared calendar and when we saw the date, we couldn't schedule anything on that day. We had to stay in PJ's all day. The PJ's were to prevent us from running out the house. It was usually on a Saturday. We get to do what we want personally for part of the day then we set a time to spend the rest of the day together.

- *__Be spontaneous.__* This is fun because you can be as creative as you want to be. I would ride the train downtown and call him to take him out for lunch. He loved when I did that and he often said it helped him break up the day and made it easier. We would role play for our sexual encounters and create a whole fun acting scene. Kiss and hug each other when your partner least expects it. Hold hands, sit together, or chase each other around the house. Yes, we did this all the time and it was so much fun!

- ***Scheduled date nights***. We believed in this before there was a name for this activity. We knew it was important to continue the fire in the relationship by dating one another. It keeps the relationship fresh and engaging.

- ***Sex is important***. Not sure what else to say here. It helps keep the passion, fire, and attraction all together. We had a lot of passion in our relationship and couldn't keep our hands off of each other. We were very private about our sex life, yet if you knew our other love languages with each other you could only imagine the heights that our sex life took us. Every single time we would want to light up a cigar and drink a glass of brandy right after kind of sex. When all the other parts of your relationship line up, you continue to want it to be at its best. SEX is the most satisfying cherry on top activity for every single act no matter how many years go by. We couldn't believe how better it got each and every time. It never got old.

- ***Talk about your dreams together.*** Every day, all day. At least for us this was daily and may have been because we both had the entrepreneurial spirit. You could speak once a week or month about it. As long as there is dialogue so that your number one supporter knows where your heart is at all times.

- ***Always celebrate your anniversary.*** This is major. To celebrate your love, pause and connect with that. Allowing time to sit with that is such a special time that you both deserve. It doesn't have to be a huge event. It could be as simple as dinner for two on your patio with candles lit.

- ***Spend time with yourself.*** Discovering who you are as an individual is constant and time must be invested in it for yourself. Why? Because you are evolving everyday, learning and growing. You both need to understand the process of what you're going through and this takes time and space. Allowing time and respect from the both of you will only enhance the time when you are together.

- ***Keep great company around your marriage***. I could preach about this until the cows come home. The company you keep has to be people that respect the union, not just one half. I'm just going to keep this all the way real. If you want the happiness you're looking for in your relationship, don't waste your time with folks that do not support your marriage or view it in a beautiful light. Lorenzo and I didn't play with this. If we had an issue within ourselves or the relationship we spoke to each other, not the world. The world doesn't care; unfortunately there are many folks that don't believe in true love and don't want you to believe in it either. What's even worse, is they don't really know what they want. This type of thinking from others causes confusion which true love does not live or thrive in. Lorenzo and I agreed from the start we would never let anyone in between us, not even our children, period.

- ***Have a high level of discretion.*** I'm so happy I was with a man that believed in this the way I did. We were known as the secretive couple and we took pride in that. There are things between a couple that stays with the couple and overtime you will learn to embrace this. Such a special way of showing love and respecting the marriage for the incredible gift that it is. Lorenzo told me he never met a woman like me that could hold secrets the way I did with him and anyone that I held close to me. He called me "Fort Knox". I'm grateful that it is a natural part of my being. Lorenzo was a very discreet person as well, so it worked between us where we knew all things were between us without saying. We knew what to share with the public; public meaning outside of us. This included our family and friends. We were never fake about our love and even had to come to the point of not hiding how we felt and treated each other. We knew many people didn't believe there could be true love and we both didn't have many examples of it. We were always authentic about our love. We just didn't air our personal chats and feelings of the world to many people, if anyone at all. We cherished our talks and private beliefs and it wasn't anyone else's business but ours. You have to get to the point to know the difference.

- ***Appreciate the quiet times.*** We could read in the same room and not say a word to each other for hours. We respected what we were into without feeling the need to have to be in each other's face the whole time. Respect the silence. So much to learn in the quietness of things. Especially about yourself.

- ***The butterfly stage.*** When we think of this stage it is usually the feelings we feel about a new relationship and all of the emotions associated with it. It feels euphoric, high-like, full of joy and happiness. Most of us love this part of a new relationship and wish it would never go away. I'm here to tell you it doesn't have to. As time goes on, the nature of the relationship will change, grow, and move into different levels. The initial feelings of the butterfly stage won't be exactly the same. Yet, you can recreate it to move through your life's purpose as a breath of fresh air. If you and your partner choose to manifest some form of a butterfly stage in your growing relationship, you can. We often forget we have the ability to choose what we want out of our relationship and shape it together to formulate an incredible and outstanding experience together.

My husband and I chased each other around the house the entire time of our relationship. It was another level of the butterfly stage. It comes in different forms and keeps the fresh feeling of sparks at all times. There wasn't a day that went by where we didn't laugh together. When you think of these small natural activities that you two let flow within the relationship, it will give you the euphoric feelings you want to keep alive between you two. I'm here to tell you we had all of that and then some. Whatever you two believe in can exist and happen for you. Does it magically appear? No. This is a constant effort on both parts to do what it takes to get what you want. The saying "you get out what you put in" is absolute with pure, true love. The biggest part of what you want lives within you. You have to put the work in yourself so you can contribute to your life's work. Marriage is a piece of art. It is a masterpiece that you and your partner are striving and working on together to create.

The Power of Love Energy

Marriage is the highest form of a union that we can have and share with the world. Lorenzo and I professed to each other on a regular basis how much we loved being married to each other. Keep in mind that as we were working on all of the parts of building a strong marriage, children were growing up and we were becoming empty nesters. We were so happy that we worked on our love in our relationship while having a child in the home. So when we became empty nesters, we didn't have to start over getting to know each other without a child. We already knew each other. We were putting in the work daily and we were showing up as the best version of ourselves and being a model for all the young people in our family including our nieces and nephews.

Young people were very important to us and we spent a lot of time with them. We knew that they looked up to us and we did everything we could to be as authentic to them as possible. We demonstrated what true love could be about and how to manage and grow individually and as a couple. The empty nester years were all that and a bag of chips and we loved it! We loved being around each other. We were very selfish about our time and it was important that we spent time with each other. Even if it meant turning down going to a party and hanging out after work. We chose each other every single day. This is one of the main reasons why we decided not to have children together because we saw early on that we really enjoyed being together and we wanted to keep that going. We already had the blended family going on and a lot of issues to sort through while being there for our family. We felt like if we really wanted to enjoy each other and go the distance for this true love magical space we had with each other, it was best for us to not have any children together.

When I reached my 40's, I wanted to have a puppy. Now don't get me wrong, Lorenzo and I had two dogs already and by this time, they had already passed away. Some years earlier, Lorenzo started his management company at an apartment site where we were residing and at that time, both of our dogs were in homes that we could visit and see as much as we wanted to. We had them both for five years before they went on and lived another five years with our family members. I always wanted a specific dog in my life since I was a little girl and that was a yorkie. My husband grew up with a yorkie and I actually met his yorkie a few years before she passed away. She happened to be his mom's dog which was bought by his father. We went back and forth and talked about getting another dog because we moved from that place and now we were living in a place that accepted pets. He wanted to give me the dog of my dreams. He had a coworker that happened to raise yorkies and he asked me if I would like a dog at this time in our lives. I said, "Yes of course!" My goodness, all my other dreams were coming true. I have my dream dog, Mia.

If you ever meet my dog or ever come around Mia or had any experiences or heard of any stories about her, you will quickly find out that Mia was our daughter. She was not a typical dog. Mia was like a little person, a little girl inside of a dog and she quickly fell in love with us, especially Lorenzo. Lorenzo was known as the dog whisperer. He speaks that language very clearly and no matter what type of dog it is, he would go up to the dog and pet the dog and the next thing you know, the dog was sitting down and doing tricks for him. He had a special quality with dogs that he acquired from his grandmother. Grandma Sims is the top dog whisperer.

Mia was the love of our life and traveled with us. She did everything with us and when we created our schedule, it was always with Mia in mind. She felt love and she knew she was loved. We were just a perfect happy family and it was a very nice life during and after our empty nester time. Mia is by far the best gift Lorenzo ever gave me. I received some very nice gifts over the past 24 years, including vehicles, lavish trips, clothing, you name it, I got it. Anytime I received a gift from my husband big or small, he would always say I deserved more and that he was going to get it for me.

The recipe referenced above with so many other sprinkles of beautiful creative ways to show love to each other each and every day will feed your soul and take you to new heights in your lives that you thought could never exist.

Testimony by Joe Battle Shauna's Nephew

Both Titi and Tio served as a continuous reminder to hold a standard for yourself. No matter what they went through, they made sure their needs were met. During their marriage, Lorenzo was like the father-in-law I always wanted. From talking business, to relaxing, and smoking my first cigar. I cherish many memories and my experience with him. I love you both!

55

Chapter 6 Part A

OUR WORLD GOT ROCKED

Lorenzo and I have practiced all of those principles consistently day in and day out. They helped us when hard times happened or when we had to pivot and find new solutions to better our lives. We tackled everything that came our way and through love and with positivity. No matter what came our way, we both remained strong and on the same page when it came to our love. We knew we still needed to nurture it, care for it, and continue to work on it no matter what was happening in the world. All of this was our saving grace for what was to come.

We were flying high in our relationship. We just couldn't believe how each day in each year that went by how much more we were in love with each other and we were excited about the future. We were especially looking forward to 2019, but even more so towards 2020 as we both had conversations about 2020 back in 2018. We spoke about how we thought our lives were going to move upwards and about how all the hard work we were putting in was going to take us to the next level. We believed all of our dreams were getting ready to fully show up.

We even had this funny joke about 2019 that he, Mia, and I were going to be the same age. I turned 49 years old in November of 2018. Lorenzo was turning 49 in April 2019. Later in 2019, Mia was set to turn 7 years old in June 2019. All three of us would be

49 years old. We thought that was just so hilarious and exciting. Life was good. 2018 was really, really good and looking back, it was also a very unique year.

Genetically, I have had premature arthritis in my knees and body since I was 25 years old. I have been told by many doctors by the time I get into my 40's that I will be looking at getting knee surgery. The doctors were a little disturbed at the fact that I was so young and couldn't quite wrap their minds around what they reviewed every time I got an X-ray. So to ease up on my joints, I was told that I had to stop riding my bike, stop skating or taking long walks. These activities pretty much came to a hard stop when I was about 42 years old and it was really hard because Lorenzo and I used to love doing these activities together.

Being creative in the activity space came easy for me when planning adventures with Lorenzo. Initially, my self-esteem took a hit and I was shaken a bit while I was in the process of recreating because I knew how much my husband loved to bike ride and do a lot of the other activities. My husband was so encouraging and loving with me. He made sure he spent time with me on the new activities, new forms of exercises, and our very extensive travel life.

Lorenzo then decided to run a triathlon, a dream of his. He was very healthy and valued eating healthy and working out consistently. He swam, rode his bike, and trained for a year. I was his cheerleader on the side line and was thrilled to be a witness watching him live out his dream.

Our travel life took off in new and elaborate directions. From experiencing standing under the Eiffel Tower, to wearing cloaks and drinking out of ice blocks at the ice bar in London, to swimming with dolphins. I just loved how we learned to adjust for each other. It's critical, especially as you both get older.

I knew my doctors were telling me the truth and I knew that I needed to adhere to it. To save my joints, I decided to take their advice and get into the swimming pool and go to some of these jazzercise classes in the water. All of my doctors agreed that my workout abilities for the rest of my days needed to be in the water because my arthritis was of the age of an 80 year old.

That meant no more running and jogging or skippy do lu, lu, lu. I had to watch myself if I wanted to keep my body functioning and going as far out as I could before I needed to do the knee surgery. In 2017, I enrolled in a water exercise class and I had a great time. I decided to go back to this class in September 2018. I only had the opportunity to go to this class one time.

When I came home from this water exercise class, I took a nap. If you know me, I'm a big time napper. I try to nap everyday and have been for over 30 plus years. I woke up feeling excruciating pain from my right leg. I couldn't walk and every part of it was strange. If I tried to stand on it. I felt like there was a waterfall gushing down my leg and I remember crying out to Lorenzo, "I need help, something is wrong! I can't walk and I believe I have internal leg bleeding." He ran to me extremely concerned, asking me what was wrong.

I said I didn't know and I started crying very hard; I'm not a crier. We were both really confused on what could possibly be going on with my leg. I calmed myself down and elevated my leg. My husband helped me ice my leg a few days later. I was hoping the pain would go away. It was very swollen so I thought maybe I did something in the water.

I contacted my doctors a few days later and told them what I felt and they thought that I did something where I inflamed my arthritis and that it may have gone up to my thigh. It wasn't uncommon for something like that to happen if it gets agitated. I kept trying to explain to my doctor that this was different. It just didn't feel like arthritis. My arthritis usually gets a little bit of pain here and there and it goes away. It's chronic, yet it comes back and forth but it doesn't stay. This pain wasn't going anywhere. So they gave me a prescription that didn't do anything for the pain.

I went another week and decided to start back with my family doctor and tell him what happened. My doctor wanted me to come in right away. He gave me all types of tests stat. He was determined to get to the bottom of what was going on with my leg. Turns out, I had a laundry list of stuff going on with my leg and I had to go see a specialist ASAP. He said indeed I was correct about my feelings and that I had internal bleeding. However, he said they just couldn't tell where the blood was coming from.

They scheduled me to see a specialist to break down what he interpreted from the MRI. Because there were at least ten things wrong. Yet, the whole time my doctors and I couldn't understand how this could have happened in a water exercise class. I was the youngest person in class. At the time I was 48 years old with a birthday in a couple of months. Meanwhile, I had to call off work. I couldn't walk. Thank goodness Lorenzo was able to work from home so he could take care of me. We were very worried. We didn't know what was going on with us and internally we both felt something strange was coming on the horizon.

During this time, Lorenzo was complaining of headaches for three weeks straight.

I noticed a little strange walk that he had, that he seemed to be quiet, and concentrating on a lot of projects. By the time we got to the third week, he was in a lot of pain. I made an executive decision and said you gotta go get checked out. Meanwhile, we're still trying to wait to see what's going to happen with my leg. The doctors and I decided to do a wait and see game. They were thinking maybe my leg could heal itself with rest. If not, surgery was the next option.

My birthday was on Thanksgiving Day in 2018. I noticed my leg turning all types of colors: purple, blue, yellow, green. I had Lorenzo take a picture of it so he could blow it up. It was sensitive to the touch. I couldn't wear any pants or stretch pants. I couldn't put a blanket on it, nor material. I didn't know what happened and it was the strangest feeling. We looked at the picture and it looked like moldy, spoiled bread. I was like holy crap my leg is infected! I gotta call the doctor.

I didn't quite make that call because as I mentioned earlier, Lorenzo was on his third week of headaches. Neither one of us wanted to be at the doctor on Thanksgiving, so we made a promise to ourselves that if he still had the headaches by Saturday, he would go in and I would make the call to the doctor about scheduling my surgery. Let me just explain to you that this whole thing was so crazy to us.

Lorenzo and I were the picture of health. We ate well, we drank our water, we took our vitamins, and we worked out. We valued good food and our sleep. We understood that all of those things were important and we needed those activities to keep us going after our dreams. The whole thing was baffling for us. It was very strange and I'll be honest with you, I was scared. I didn't know what was going on. It was just so out of sorts for us and frankly not supposed to happen to us.

Saturday came. Lorenzo still had headaches and my leg was still in shades of colors. So we had to be the man and woman of our word and suck it up and head to the emergency room. We carried our notebooks, books, laptops and stopped to grab something to eat. We wanted to make sure we were prepared for anything that came our way. We stopped at Bruegger's Bagel. I love that place. They make a mean tuna fish sandwich with heated melted cheese on a rosemary bagel. Okay let me get my mind away from food because I love to eat!

Meanwhile, I leaned on Renz and hopped into the car. Since I couldn't walk, he said he'll go in and get our order. I told him I'll write it down for you because I just kind of noticed that his head was kind of all over the place and he wasn't really himself the last few weeks. He left for 15 minutes. I'm thinking wow there must be a lot of people in there. He comes back to the car, closes the door right away, looks at me in my face and says, "Take me to the hospital right now." I'm like, "What happened, what's the matter, where is the food? "He said, "I didn't get it." I asked why. He said because he got up to the line and the lady asked him how can I help you and he looked at her. He said to himself he had no clue why he was in there, what he was getting, and what was going on.

I'm so grateful that he knew where the truck was because I'm thinking, "Oh my God!" I wrote down the order and all he had to do was read it. Let me tell you about Lorenzo. He was a highly intelligent man, a person that memorized lines, speeches, and managed millions of dollars of real estate for the company he worked for. We both looked at each other and we got out of there quickly. We went to the hospital and headed straight for the emergency room to sign in.

The nurse at the counter walked up with a wheelchair for me. I said to him we are here for my husband. The nurse looked at me and said you look like you need a wheelchair. They took Lorenzo in the back and they quickly ran an MRI on him because he had trouble remembering his birthday and the year. Then, the crazy part was that he looked at me and said, "I know that's not the year. Why did I say that? I can't remember my birthday! This is crazy, Shauna. What's going on?" I told him I don't know why and we were there to find out.

They admitted him ASAP and said he had to see a specialist on Monday and that they were not releasing him until Monday morning. They wouldn't tell us what they saw in the MRI, they just said that they saw some masses and that the specialist had to be the one to interpret. I'm frantic about his head and my leg is a hot mess. We didn't know what was going on with him and he displayed some signs that were not in character. I knew this wasn't his style, but my intuition told me to call a few family members to let them know what was going on. Although we were a very discreet couple, something felt strange about this situation. Lorenzo really wasn't that happy about me doing it but later on he thanked me for it. Sometimes you just have to do what's best for each other when one person is going through it. We believed in that as a couple and we made the choice to stay as positive as possible with any outcomes.

On Monday morning, we saw the specialist. It was in a large hospital so I was in a wheelchair. Lorenzo had to push me to his appointment and you could imagine how that looked. We both looked at each other and laughed about it. I mean what else could we do but make light of the situation as best as we could.

As we entered the office of the cancer neurologist specialist, the specialist looked at both of us. Then he said, "I see a male's name that I'm supposed to see today but I'm looking at you young lady and I'm trying to figure out who is the patient here." Again, Renz and I looked at each other and laughed. This whole thing felt like the Twilight Zone. Then Lorenzo spoke up and said, "I'm the patient."

The specialist said he would talk to him in a second and looked at me and said, "What's going on with you young lady?" I said I actually have an appointment and talked to the doctors that morning. They scheduled surgery for me right away so I was going to have surgery Wednesday in this same hospital. Perplexed as he was looking at us, he turned to Lorenzo and asked him to step into another room where he had his MRI scans up on the computer. They were gone for a few minutes and Renz returned telling me they had the wrong guy with the wrong charts. Now I'm confused looking at the doctor. The doctor said my husband had seven masses in the back of his head from ear to ear. He said he didn't know what it was. He didn't want to alarm us, but that it was serious and they needed to do a biopsy to see. He said he would have done it that day if he could schedule him in. The closest appointment he could get was Friday of that week. In four days he had to have the surgery biopsy and in two days I was getting my leg cut from the bottom of the knee to my upper thigh to get out the infection I was feeling in my leg.

Testimony by Jha'Tier Robinson, Shauna's Niece

The reason I know true unconditional love exists is because of the love shared between my Titi and Tio. Their story is one that has influenced so many in life and after; mine especially. I am eternally grateful to be a witness.

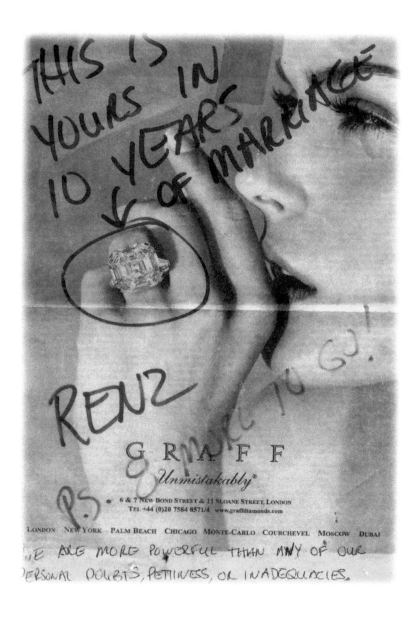

Chapter 6 Part B

OUR WORLD GOT ROCKED

Continues...

My surgery was the Wednesday of that week. We packed our bags and Lorenzo stayed in the room with me. I'm fighting back my tears while I'm writing this. The nursing staff brought us an extra bed for Renz so that he could sleep next to me. This was the first time we ever slept in separate beds in our marriage. It was a very strange feeling.

We held hands and just gazed into each other's eyes. We read each other's mind and knew no matter what happened we would make the best of the situation. After the surgery, I was totally out of it. I was on a lot of medication and had a huge cast around my leg. I couldn't tell you my name. I knew where I was, I knew what had happened, but I was totally wiped out. I had to ring a bell for the nurse for anything that I needed. I had no choice but to use a bedpan. It was a very humbling experience to say the least. Next up, was Lorenzo's biopsy on Friday.

When Lorenzo had his biopsy, I couldn't be there for him. It was the worst. I couldn't see straight and I was in so much pain. I had my niece, Jha, prepare Lorenzo's overnight bag and make sure all of his paperwork was together. He literally had his biopsy two floors away from me. I was dealing with my own agony, pain, and breakdown and I couldn't be there for him. This was so insane.

After a couple of days of observation, they released Lorenzo. He couldn't stay at the hospital any longer. He seemed like he was in a bit of a shock from everything and needed to go home. I stayed the rest of that week and then I got papers to move to a rehab hospital. I was wheelchair bound and had to depend on the nursing staff to care for me. I spent a month in a rehab hospital and in that month I felt so lonely. I couldn't help my husband and he couldn't help me. He was at home taking some time for himself. He took some days off of work to try to figure out the results of this biopsy and to visit me at the rehab hospital.

Each time he visited, I could see him slipping into a different person. I just couldn't understand what was going on and I couldn't wait for the results because the change I was seeing in my husband was moving fast. I had a picc line in my arm. I had to have various medications infused every four hours and was forced to sleep on my back. I'm not a back sleeper so this was torturous for me. Sleepless nights are the worst.

My son and Jha learned how to administer the medication in my picc line while I was in rehab so that they could care for me at home. I was still in a wheelchair even after all of the therapy with my leg that was OMG so painful to move an ounce. They decided I was good enough to go home and have outpatient therapy in my home. Meanwhile, I was so worried about my husband at this point. We were still waiting to hear back from the specialist about his biopsy results.

Observing Renz and some changes I witnessed let me know I had to get well and as fast as possible. My son, niece and Aunt D. moved in with us to help. My Aunt D. was a former registered nurse. We all had no idea what was going on and where we were all heading as a family. The day that I got released from the rehab hospital and my family moved in, Lorenzo had an appointment the very next day to get the results.

We all made the decision that Renz couldn't be behind the wheel until we understood what was going on with him, therefore my son drove him. It was a bit of a tussle, a bit of a struggle because Renz didn't want to give up the idea of not being able to drive himself. We just wanted him to be safe. When they returned from the appointment, the first thing Lorenzo said was, "We're going to talk about this one time and then we're not going to talk about this anymore." I said, "Okay, no problem." He was clearly upset by the news and I'm holding on, in bed trying to wrap my mind around what they were getting ready to tell me.

My husband had what they called Glioblastoma. It is the granddaddy of brain tumors. A mystical ugly tumor that has no cure. It's not genetic and it's not from the environment. It grows inside of a person. Whatever this was, it took a cell in his brain and caused a mutation in which it started controlling his brain. It then moves pretty quickly to shutting down parts of the brain that controls the mind and the body and it does it at a rapid pace. Lorenzo was scheduled for another appointment the following week for him to make a decision on how he wanted to approach this dilemma.

He asked me if I would be mad at him if he didn't do chemo. He said that he didn't want to because there wasn't a cure and he didn't want to go through the pain and weakness associated with it. He told me that he wanted to be at home. I told him that I couldn't make the decision for him. This was his life and he had to decide what he wanted to do. In the same breath, I mentioned whatever he decided I had his back 110%.

Before we could even make that appointment, Lorenzo had a seizure; the first of three. I was in the living room on the phone speaking to my nurse about my leg and trying to let them know that I couldn't be an outpatient because my husband had a serious diagnosis and I have to be here for him. My nurse was on the phone at the time trying to remind me that I still had to take care of myself. I let my nurse know that I would indeed take care of myself and do the therapy that they wanted me to do, but that they needed to bring the therapy to meet me in my home because I wasn't leaving my husband's side. They were able to make that arrangement.

While we were speaking about it on the phone, I heard Jha distressfully from the bedroom. She was visiting her Tio and speaking to him as he was watching Netflix. He had a seizure. My nurse heard this through the phone and started giving us techniques on what to do. I shouted to my niece because I was inclined in our recliner and unable to get up or walk.

We called 911. They arrived right away! My niece was so on top of it! She was able to give a very detailed description how it started, what was happening, and for how long. I sent my niece to go into the ambulance with her uncle. I couldn't possibly move fast at all. I got dressed and packed a bag for both of us because I didn't know what this was going to turn into. We were in the thick of uncharted waters and both of us were clueless on what our future looked like. We were both really nervous at this point. When I got to the hospital, I had to be pushed in my wheelchair. He was out of it. I

70

never saw him like that. He was totally, totally out of it. Lorenzo ended up being hospitalized for almost a week. I just couldn't understand what was going on. Why was this happening?

The hospital happened to be full that night. There was a lot going on. They didn't have a room for Renz yet. We remained in the emergency room; which felt like forever. They couldn't send him back home. They also contacted his doctors in the cancer research area so they were all aware of what just happened to Lorenzo.

A room finally became available. My family was so happy to get out of the emergency room. I was being pushed in a wheelchair praying, meditating, and asking God what was going on. When we reached the floor, I felt like I was in a dazed state. We stopped. They pushed his hospital bed into a room that felt familiar and a bit eerie to me. I looked up and said to myself, "What the hell?"

Remember when I was in the hospital for a week when they cut my leg? This was my room. I had the best nursing staff and the best doctors. I felt blessed to be on that floor after my first leg surgery. I looked up Lorenzo in the same room that I was in a month before where they rolled a hospital bed for him next to mine. Where I was in so much pain and I couldn't talk. Where the picc line that is still in my arm was placed. Two floors up from where Renz had his biopsy.

This time they're rolling a bed next to him for me. We switched places. How weird is this? We both looked at each other, shook our heads, and could only laugh out loud. What else could we do? Each doctor and nurse stopped in their tracks when they saw us. They could not believe, understand, or comprehend why Lorenzo was in the hospital. Next thought for them was why was I in the bed next to him? It was a shock to everybody.

I joked with the staff and said that I was five months older than him. He likes to do everything I do. Everyone laughed, including Lorenzo. We did the best we could to make light of the fact; even though we both knew that we were facing something serious. They ran all types of tests on him. There was one where they had to place electric needle-like items all over his head. It poked in his scalp and he was not okay with it. He was trying to pull it out of his head. I'm in the bed next to him. I can't move. I'm trying to call the nurse. I'm like, "You're gonna hurt yourself, you can't do this, we gotta get through this together." I finally got a hold of the doctors and told them they have to take all of this off of him now or he will take it out himself. He is not having this. If you know my husband personally, restrictions of any kind is not his thing.

The staff stopped what they were doing and unhooked this contraption they had on his head. They sent his cancer doctor down to talk to us a few hours later. He was very direct and frank with us. He said he was going to give us five hours to think about our decision. He told Lorenzo this is very serious. He said these masses were going to end up succumbing and taking over his life and he needed to try to do chemo although there was no cure and no guarantees to save his life. After 5 hours, he came back with a team of doctors.

When the doctor started informing us on the number of days Renz would have to be at the hospital every week for chemo, I could see in Lorenzo's eyes he had already checked out on this idea. Lorenzo's mind was made up. He politely listened to the team of doctors that were in his room pleading their case. They all admitted they've never seen Glioblastoma this aggressive in a person specifically in Lorenzo's age group. After all of that, Lorenzo asked for five minutes to speak with me alone. He said, "Shauna, I'm not doing it. I'm not going to be a guinea pig. I'm going to watch my Netflix and whatever is supposed to happen. I made my peace with it." I cried like a baby. As always I expressed to him that I support whatever decision he makes.

Lorenzo had a brilliant mind. It doesn't surprise me that he was able to manage this illness for as long as he did without his knowledge of it. He shook all of the doctor's hands and thanked them for what they've done for him. Then he said I'm going home to watch Netflix.

I felt so lost and yet so comforted by God's hands. There was this overwhelming feeling like God was scooping us up and doing something with us. That he wanted the world to witness our journey. I couldn't focus on that at all. All I cared about at that moment was that something was majorly wrong and that it was beyond our control. We both didn't care for this feeling.

After he told the team of doctors how he felt, he then nodded his head. He was happier than a lark about the fact that he was going home. I felt frozen and numb to all of this. They ended up moving us down to an end corner with a bigger room with a nice view because we had all types of family and friends come through. He preferred to see family and friends at the hospital if possible because he told me we're not having a rodeo at the house. My response was of course not. We never rolled like that and we are not going to start now. I called as many people as I could to come by to see him. We stayed a couple more days while the hospital connected us with hospice care to initiate the home experience that Lorenzo wanted for himself. I was still a wreck. Not knowing what was to come and dealing with my pain in my leg as well. When the paperwork was completed, we were discharged to go home and begin hospice care.

Testimony by Aniya Wall, Shauna's Niece

What I admire most about my Tio and Titi's love was the way they treated each other. Tio was Titi's king and she was his queen. No one will ever love Titi the way my Tio did. Funny story, whenever we would come over to their home and watch movies together, Titi would always pause the movie and try to explain to us about what was going on. Tio would be like, "Shauna let the kids watch the movie." We would all laugh as a family together.

Chapter 7

WE REMAIN HOLDING HANDS

Hospice started Christmas of 2018. Hospice life was like no other life I've ever experienced or witnessed. I had family and friends that are in the nursing industry say what Lorenzo and I went through was something that elderly people experience. That it wasn't normal for us to be experiencing this and all of the stresses that were associated with it.

Renz and I always held hands and we held them even more just at home in our bedroom. We gazed into each other's eyes and without speaking knew what we both felt. We were so wrapped up into each other's souls it really was a thing of beauty. Holding his hand was always special to me from the start.

The first gentlemen that ever showed me love in such a simple way without words. I was always moved and it never got old. Renzo and I always stayed in the present when we were together. Hospice life was no different. We continued our fun-loving ways and remained in tune with one another.

This life was a beast. I was still in a wheelchair and doing therapy everyday at home. I was working so hard just to stand and take a step. It was very painful and OMG mentally challenging for me. All the while, I'm watching this thing start taking over my husband's life. Glioblastoma is an ugly thing. We did our best to still enjoy our days. Our first month of hospice was strange because he seemed so great, we laughed a lot and re-watched movies that we both enjoyed together. I really truly believed that we could beat this. We thought we would be the first ones to beat Glioblastoma and we would write books, tour the country, host seminars and speeches on how we did it. We were the Hibbitts and the Hibbitts were strong and they never let adversity or challenges get them down.

Our family motto is there were never any problems, there were only solutions. We had short conversations over movies, memories, and our life together. He would periodically ask me if everything was okay with the bills and the budget. I would think to myself there goes Mr. Finance, still concerned about taking excellent care of us in his time of need. I love him. I always let him know that everything was under control and that he didn't have anything to worry about. I had one good cry that hit me and I laid across his body when it happened. He caressed my hair and head and told me everything was going to be okay. He said that everything will always work out at the end. We then looked at each other and said this part together, "It always does".

I really thought we could beat this according to his behavior and attitude in January...until February. I don't like to think about what happened in February 2019, but for the sake of this book I have to. I saw such a quick downturn in February. I saw a man be able to manage himself in January and not be able to manage himself in February. This was the month he stopped talking. This was the month my heart ached tremendously. It was our personal favorite holiday together...Valentines Day. I had to think of something creative even though we both were living in our bedroom. I texted my neighbor, Jackie, to see if she could pick up a dozen roses for us. Jackie and her mom picked out a very stunning dozen roses and delivered them to our door. When I placed them in a vase and put them in our bedroom, Renz exhibited a huge smile and gave me two thumbs up. This was a very humble and emotional moment for the both of us.

After half of February was over, Lorenzo started sleeping all day from sun up to sun down. I had to wake him up to eat and take his meds. He ate very well and never missed a meal. He also consistently took his meds. This thing had gotten so heavy on him that all he could do was sleep. The precious thing about it was that he wasn't in pain, he was just tired. I ended up buying a video monitor with a camera so that I could watch him and make sure he was okay. Since his first seizure, I always made sure someone was close by if it happened again. It indeed happened again. Fortunately, I was able to catch it from the start on camera from the kitchen and was able to get back to the room as quickly as possible.

When I entered the room with him, his whole body shook from head to toe and he had no idea what was happening. He kept looking at me. I kept looking at him and just trying to keep his body calm. When it stopped he looked at me and I looked at him. I asked him if he was alright. He nodded his head yes and he went back to sleep. Every day from that day forward, I went into the living room to pray and cry. It was so stressful. There is no way I was going to lose the best person that ever walked into my life. No way.

Lorenzo was very concerned about me and wanted to make sure I was good. So I decided that I would do all my crying in the other room. He couldn't see what I was witnessing because I didn't want to alarm him.

The Power of Love Energy

March 2019 came in with another crazy seizure. The seizure took away some of Renz's abilities and he needed more help from myself and the hospice team. The level of care, love and support from The Hospice of the Western Reserve is hard to put into words. The best thing I could say is they clearly got it. No matter how many clients they had and who they worked with, they understood the human aspect of the stresses and the trauma of what was happening in one's home. They respected the intimacy that surrounded the trauma and I am forever grateful for them.

On March 24, 2019, Lorenzo was dealing with a lot of breathing complications. He was experiencing what they call in the medical field "cheyne stokey". It is a heavy breathing sound that is interrupted by complete silence, stops, and pauses of the breath. I was scared because I was already warned that it was usually a sound that's heard before the person transitions. The hospice team sent a counselor to speak to me about where we were in the process of Lorenzo's health about a week prior. They told me that eventually, naturally the body would start shutting down and that it was very painful. They mentioned that I would need to make the decision to give him morphine and whenever I decide to, I had to remember two things. One, that I am not doing anything wrong and to work hard to not feel guilty when that time comes. Two, morphine accelerates the transition. With deep sadness, I had to make the executive decision to administer and start him on morphine soon after hospice talked to me.

He stopped eating for a couple of days and you could tell he was experiencing a different type of feeling in his body. I saw him in discomfort and major pain for the first time. I cried every time I gave him the morphine although I knew I was doing the right thing. I never wanted him to suffer and I didn't want him to be in pain.

78

They say you can feel guilty about having to make that decision. I don't feel guilty at all. I took excellent care of him with every part of my being. I fulfilled the ultimate love you could give to your spouse and that is loving and caring for them to death do you part. I asked God for one thing, whatever happens, please let me be with him when he takes his last breath. I didn't want to be in a kitchen, a doctor's appointment or even in therapy in the next room. Just with him.

God granted me that prayer and I am forever grateful. I held his hand as he breathed heavier and heavier. I hugged him and I kissed him. I told him nothing in this world could ever separate our love because I would love him forever and I will catch up with him. He looked at me and he took his last breath while I was holding his hand on March 24, 2019. Right now writing this, I'm crying. Words cannot explain the pain…it's indescribable.

No one could tell me in a million years I would lose my husband right before his 49th birthday. It didn't make sense. Why was I going through this? This was a bad dream I desperately wanted somebody to wake me up from.

I cried from the depths of my soul; sounds I've never heard my body ever make. I cried so deep I sounded like a wounded animal. I felt like every part of my flesh had been cut and carved out. My mind was all over the place and I couldn't grasp what we've just gone through. Zoned out in this space, somehow I was able to plan his homegoing, write the program, and organize my thoughts.

I worked with his masonic brothers and sisters from his Masonic Lodge Excelsior #11 and Queen Elizabeth (the sister organization to the Masonic Lodge). They all assist me with Renz's personal ceremony. Yes, I had to sit through two ceremonies. One on Friday and one on Saturday. I always knew about this process when we were much younger. Lorenzo would always speak so highly about having a masonic funeral. He would apologize to me in advance for sending me through this. Yet, he was always excited to know he would be honored in such a beautiful way.

Here I am trying to take the time to figure out how we got here in the five short months after I injured my leg. My husband complained of headaches. We both had surgery and we started hospice. I lost my husband before I could learn how to walk again. WTF! WTF! WTF! WTF! WTF! times a million. I felt like I was having a heart attack and I wanted to die immediately. Nothing mattered in that moment to me.

Lorenzo's homegoing celebration was the most magnificent send off I have ever witnessed. Through all of my tears, I kept thanking God because I knew he knew best. I was numb, extremely numb. I had no knowledge of life outside of myself. I went through the motions of the two ceremonies. I had to sit still feeling so grateful for every visitor that was present or for those that wanted to be there and couldn't. It was quite a crowd, my husband was so loved.

I wrote a letter and it was printed in the program. I wasn't sure if I would be able to read it. I had my best friend since I was 12 years old, Cynthia, standby in case I couldn't read the letter. I have no clue how I did it. My son went up to the podium with me and I read the letter. I looked out into the crowd for a few moments. My eyes were so heavy, my heart ached, and I was just in this awful dream. Walking passed his beautiful body, sleeping like an angel. This couldn't be real. I begged for it not to be real.

Deep down, I felt like I waited for Lorenzo to return: hoping he was just away on a work trip. I didn't want to accept this. It was really too much to bear. I couldn't hold my head up and I didn't want to eat much. The amount of family support around me was priceless. My family and I knew we had to take our time to process what we all have been through and figure out what was next for us. Lorenzo was the patriarch of our young family and he imparted so much to each of us. We were devastated and frankly, torn to pieces as a whole. I was not sure what was to come as I went over all of our dreams and our lives together. We were so young and in love for so long. We grew up together. Learning about ourselves in our 20's, 30's, and 40's. I dread to think what was next.

I do have a confession to make that I was unable to share with Renz for fear that it would come true. I have always worried about Lorenzo passing away at a young age ever since I met him. It was only because his mother passed away at a young age and he had many family members pass at a young age as well. When he turned 40 years old I was relieved. Why? Because his mother was 39 years old when she transitioned. I thought if he turns 40, we will be home free and we will make it to our 80's like we're supposed to. Unfortunately, the graveyard shift Renz always spoke about when he told others about our relationship happened.

I felt like all of this was cut too short and in a way it felt extremely unfair. I had a great life with a man that loved my quirkiness, my artsy fartsy ways as he would call it, intellect, inner and outer beauty, my crazy thoughts, randomness, creativity, free spiritedness and serial entrepreneurial tendencies. WHO THE F*** IS GOING TO GET THAT? I'm a puzzle made up of so many parts who loves the world and wants nothing more but to give back my skills and talents to the world. I feel like no one will get me the way Lorenzo got me. He and I believed in soul mates and we recognized it early in our relationship that we were experiencing this in the here and now. Half of me was gone. I felt like half of my brain was gone. I couldn't think, sleep, function and not to mention, still couldn't walk. All the anxiety I had that surrounded that. I couldn't believe this was happening to me.

The life Lorenzo and I experienced could not be all for nothing? There has to be something bigger. Our love was bigger. What I know in my soul is that all the answers will unfold as time goes on. Right now I have to dig deep, and find a way to heal without feeling guilty for doing it. I say it like that because grief robs us of so many things…at first.

Testimony by Art Ledger IV, Shauna's Nephew

My Tio's and Titi relationship was like the ideal love everybody wants to experience. The way they cared for each other, you would think they knew each other from before birth. We learned A LOT from them. They showed me you are supposed to be completely yourself with another person and never be judged. They taught me the smarter way around things instead of just doing it. There's a lot more, but what I take with me everyday is the love my Tio had for my Titi and his family.

CHAPTER 8

WHAT NOW?

I was not feeling this. You could take this experience and shove it somewhere. I asked God to bring him back. I cried loudly for weeks that I would do anything to have him back. I pleaded to give me another chance. I felt like I was being punished for something I didn't do. I couldn't wrap my mind, spirit around this at all. I didn't like it and I couldn't take it anymore. I wanted someone to stop the excruciating pain. Over and over, I thought, "Why am I here? Why don't I just go where he is? Yes! That is right! I want to go with him so I don't have to feel. So, I am not apart from him." We were supposed to be together. It was bullshit. A bunch of nonsense and I needed this stupid shit to stop ASAP!!!!!!

Yet, the pain kept dragging me through a series of emotions. I felt like I was being dragged with no conscience of my whereabouts. It was a very dark time for me. As if it wasn't enough pain I immediately entered his birthday and our anniversary. All together packaged up to pump more pain inside of me. To continue to paralyze me. The worst part was I couldn't do anything about it. I had to force myself to feel the emotions and go through the struggle of understanding how this grief shit works.

I woke up to WTF now pain. Renz's 49th birthday on April 11th, five days after the homegoing. REALLY!!!!!!!!!!!!!! That's the way this is going to play out? As if I didn't get enough!!! Why would I have to endure all of this at this particular time and space?

The gratitude I have for my family is beyond words. They helped me celebrate Renz's Birthday by releasing balloons at his gravesite at 4:11 pm on April 11th. Lorenzo and I both loved the fact that we shared the #11 together.

My birthday is 11/22. We thought it was a neat connection between us. I would tell him he was born on that day because he always knew the 411. We would both get a kick out of that and we even had an apartment number 411 at one time.

Meanwhile, we interrupt this amazing memory to get back to the bullshit…grief. It is always there. It is going nowhere. It needs a home and not here. This was not the spot. I was not its brother's keeper.

I threw up daily in my notebook. I called my GRIEF THROW-UP. It was notes I captivated from what was happening to me. I wanted to someday look back and see where I was then, and how I could best describe the way grief had a grip on me.

My idea of a grief throw up page was a way for me to acknowledge and connect with my true feelings. This was the rawest and most vulnerable time ever in my life. Like a snapshot, I came up with these emotions and told myself not to be ashamed or afraid of what I write. I knew it would help me therapeutically if I let it flow. So I did just that. If you've ever lost a close loved one, you may be able to relate to some of the crazy shit and random thoughts that come to one's mind when they are going through the grieving stages.

Now I pause here to take a moment to write out my emotions. To respect each emotion as valid. To usher zero judgments to those thoughts. To honor my feelings. To figure out how to acknowledge them and move on. To not give it power over my life. To sit with the thoughts. To move through them. To forgive myself if the thoughts were super crazy to the human mind. Ladies and gentlemen here is my raw truth of emotions. My grief throw-up page.

My eyelashes hurt.

I have a busted blood vessel in one of my eyes…it's still there.

There is no joy in my eyes or joy in the fake smile I'm flashing from time to time.

I don't care to meet anyone new…not a neighbor, friend, no one. If you don't know Mr. Hibbitts you missed out big time. There is no need for us to get to know each other. My life has ended.

I'm just going to drink this away.

I know, I know I'll just sleep it away.

You know what…fuck it I'll stay inside for the rest of my life and watch TV there is nothing else to do.

How can I numb this pain…someone give me the answer…I can't breathe.

Dammit I said I CAN'T BREATHE!!!!!!!!!!!!!!!

The Power of Love Energy

I feel trapped.

I'm sick…I feel very ill.

Food doesn't taste the same.
This is the worst, Stop the fuckin game already I give up.

Going to crawl over to the gravesite and yep dig him up and lay myself down with him. Now that's a great idea!

Don't care about Summer.

Don't care about the end of this love story.

Knock me out, I'll come back in another lifetime. I have to catch up with Mr. Hibbitts.

I used to be the one that loved to eat…now I'm eating to live.

My California king size bed where are you Renz?

Reaching my arms out to him, feeling his presence…his spirit is so incredibly powerful.

It wasn't his time. It wasn't our time.

I don't like this.

Please stop the bleeding if anyone cares please stop the bleeding. Please don't tell me you understand if you have no clue what it's like to lose a spouse and especially losing your soul-mate.

Now it's time to take a cry break.

Testimony by Marquetta Abdul-Wali, Shauna's Cousin

I witnessed Lorenzo and Shauna's love. They had drive, loyal companionship, an inspiring love for travel, and a flare of royalty. That is what keeps me in the remembrance of King Lorenzo and Queen Shauna.

Chapter 9

MY GRIEF WALK

As I walked down the grim hall of grief, it often reminded me I was in hell. This grief walk made my skin feel dry and tight as if it was winter everyday. Flashes of dark tunnels with no light or end at sight. Winter is my least favorite season and I felt like I was stuck there. Dark and gloomy. This was not normal nor cool. It was so dark here.

I immediately withdrew within myself really trying to find out what exactly happened. Frankly, how could I change it? There must be a way because I never thought in my wildest dreams that I would lose Lorenzo period. We often spoke about death and I would say I was going first. He would tell me he couldn't live without me therefore he is going first. He would tell me I was strong and could handle his death better than he could handle mind. All this doesn't matter. What mattered was that this was all too soon for us. The graveyard shift was supposed to go to our eighties. He was only 48 and I was 49 years old. This is not the way our lives were supposed to go.

Not only did we have more living to do, we were still chasing after our dreams together. I lived the greatest life a woman could ever live in this lifetime with my soul mate. I remember saying to myself one day out loud, "Okay Renz, stop with the games and bring your behind back here ASAP."

The Power of Love Energy

Now I'm trapped with my life-sentence. This is by far my hardest and most difficult loss to date. This was a new thing for me and for many of my family members. How or what do I do? Who would I talk to? I was totally lost and not to mention had to look forward to a second leg surgery so they could force-bend my leg. Really???? I couldn't think about that. The way I was hurting it was not something I could even entertain. I knew I had to take care of myself. I just needed time to breathe. The last five months were ridiculous and I owed it to myself to take the time to sit with it all. I was literally suffocating and it was a bunch of malarkey at that point to me. I felt like I was in the twilight zone. Crying for hours, days, and weeks on end. My eyelashes hurt. I felt each individual hair on my eyelid screaming and asking for the pain to stop. It felt like I was getting punched all day everyday. The abuse that life handed me was unfair and I had no conscious of what it was doing to me. I felt defeated and destroyed.

I remain inwards trying to devise a plan while learning how to honor my feelings at the same time. Everyone grieves differently and it is not up to anyone on how a person should feel or behave. We are individuals and therefore have to individually grieve the best way it feels to us. At the same time, I've been a teacher, and I knew those around me had to be educated on how to handle me. I was fragile and had to walk the walk of a widow alone next to my family. The agony it gave me to watch my family witness this new "Shauna" was the worst. I really didn't like watching my son see his powerful, inspired mother broken, lost, and afraid. What was I afraid of? Doing this beautiful thing called life without Renz. My mind couldn't fathom the thought.

This person, who had been through a traumatic experience, whose core was shook was not me. Who was I? Why did God and the universe pick me to do this job to care and love such a special person? Where would I go from here? These questions were in my mind over and over again. I knew in order to be healthy I had to go real slow, develop a plan that I felt would work for me, and stay focused on my overall well-being.

The Cleveland Hospice of the Western Reserve reached back out to me after their incredible services that Renz and I experienced at home before his transition. They offered me bereavement counseling. Saying yes to that forever changed my life and got me started on the road to recovery. I also have to mention and thank from the bottom of my heart my therapist. Thank you so much Mary Murphy from the Bereavement Coordinator of the Western Reserve. Mary helped me dig deep to figure out what made me happy. You allowed me the time needed to do this. I will forever be grateful for you.

I discovered early on in my grief walk that I had to do things that made me feel good. One of my loves is travel. Renz coined yet another nickname for me "Will Travel". My travel life started in my early childhood years. From road trips with the family, flying back and forth to Puerto Rico, to later becoming an exchange student in Japan by age 16. I'm connected to an amazing Japanese family that loves me and still communicates with me to this day. I've been fortunate enough to have visited them a total of four times in my lifetime. I plan on many more in the future. The peace that I get from their culture is priceless and I am glad I have a hold of it because that's what I need to make it on this grief journey.

So I spoke with my therapist and asked her if I could start with phone calls because I was going to travel and seek answers for myself. This was my way of pausing and connecting with myself to see what life was speaking to me at such a vulnerable time in my life. She said it was no problem. Therefore, I bounced with my cane in tow and wheelchair requests for travel.

Phoenix was a great start for me- I started counseling sessions with Mary after my first stop to Phoenix at a resort that was full of peace and beauty. My best friend Cynthia and my niece Jha came with me so that I wasn't alone. They both so eloquently let me be in the manner that I needed. They allowed me to do whatever I wanted to do. After all, we were all grieving together. It was a beautiful time being still, eating fantastic food, and chilling in a cabana area poolside. It was everything my internal doctor ordered. I also was visited by my family that resided there, my cousin Anthony, his wife Tracy, my cousin IIcia, her husband Roberto, and my Titi Becky. This was the cherry on top. Visiting Phoenix and being at that resort reminded me of how beautiful life is. It was a nice, slowed down version of watching nature and becoming one with it. *Next up, New York Brooklyn Style-* I have a male cousin that is more like my brother. BJ has the intellect of a human that has been on this earth thousands of times. He developed a great relationship with my husband to the point they conversed on the phone without my involvement. He came home to Cleveland pretty regularly and was there for me like a rock during this whole ordeal. My niece Jha and I flew to stay with him and his beautiful wife Didem in Brooklyn. This was a very special trip for me. It was the first time I felt my husband with me the entire time. My husband's presence was very strong and he was in the midst. We all felt him. One of my favorite activities in New York was the picnic his wife planned for us. We enjoyed listening to music on YouTube for hours, taking turns choosing a different song to share with the group. Again, we were all in this together. We felt each other's pain and did everything to try to honor each other's feelings. We poured into one another. This trip was everything and gave me food for thought on how to pivot for my future. I felt an energy of love, compassion, and peace that was rushed upon me from head to toe. Although I was sad, I was happy to be sad with my family. They get me.

The many flavors of Chicago- This trip was preplanned four years ago prior to Renzo's passing. One of our nephews, Dererk Pardon, was graduating from North Western University. Lorenzo was super excited about this coming up as each year passed by. Our nephew played on the men's basketball team and was a superstar on and off the court. We loved his humbleness and intellect and how he always showed us love while he was on his life's purpose and journey. I will admit this was a hard trip for me because of all the excitement Renz and I had for this day. I had moments where I physically stopped. Like when we were heading to my nephew's agent house to watch the game, everyone waited for me outside the van as I collected myself to proceed.

It was a beautiful weekend, the weather was perfect. Watching my nephew graduate from such a prestigious school was the best feeling from that trip. The second best moment was when my nephew made brunch reservations at a restaurant directly across the street from Wrigley Field. This particular moment I made sure that I stepped out of grief and remained present for that experience. It doesn't come by too often in life. I had the best time through my sadness and worked hard to smile and show my appreciation to the universe. All through this, I remained extremely grateful.

Vegas what happens in Vegas stays in Vegas- I know you're probably thinking of how Vegas comes into play? Well this was an excursion. My nephew was selected to play in the Summer League for the Orlando Magic. I love the lifestyle of basketball, the game, fashion, music, the whole thing. There was no way I wasn't going to watch him play. This was a very important step in his career. Vegas was good to me because I've been there seven times with Renz. The first time I ever went to Vegas was when we got married. I have the best memories with Lorenzo in Vegas. Although this was the first time without him, I was happy to be there.

After my trip to Vegas, I returned home to Cleveland. It was time to pack and go through Lorenzo's items. I found every time I returned to the apartment after a trip. I got really depressed. I was offered to stay in the building and get a smaller apartment. I almost went for this until I realized I couldn't even walk our dog Mia. Everywhere I looked in my beautiful neighborhood that Renz and I lived in the last 12 years all of a sudden became painful to look at. I couldn't even go to the grocery store. I continued shopping from the app and picking groceries up to avoid the pain of facing all the fun conversations he and I had in the store together.

We made all boring errands into an adventure, and there was always laughter and private chats. We both loved our love and our strong bond. We knew it was extraordinary and we both knew we deserved to feel good about our love because we put constant work into building it up so it would overflow. We basked in our love. As Renz would say, "All day, every day."

After deep meditations, I made the decision to move from our current neighborhood. It was seriously hurting my soul. I couldn't take it nor afford more beat downs to my spirit. I packed, went through everything for a few days, planned the move, and found a new place to stay in between all of my grief trips. It was the only way I could do it. My family helped me and I had a very special neighbor Rotaunja that gave hours and days of her time to help me get through it all. Thank you so much. You know who you are and what that meant to me. I was still on a cane struggling to walk while trying to reposition myself, soul search, and plan for a second operation on my leg at the end of the summer. Ayyyyy yaiiii yaiiii! Writing this all still has me in shock of how I was able to get through that summer!

Atlanta, ATL in the house- I have to take a moment and just say how grateful I am to have family around the world that loves me. It is a very special space to be in in this lifetime. As you can see I have a large family and am connected to so many of them; especially, my cousins. I have a special place in my heart for them. Thank you to my Ledger and Ortiz family!

Watching beautiful life around me at a time when I was going through an ugly process was necessary. The problem was it was only moments of relief from the grief. I did everything I could to control this but often failed because at the end of the day, for me to get stronger I had to feel all the feels. I had to tell myself, "It's okay, this is normal, you will make it through and take your time to heal." In my case, it was my mind, body, and soul that required my full attention. As much as I love life, all things summer, and celebrations, I had to go through my process and not rush it. If I rushed it, I may not have ever gotten to a strong healing space. The thought of that scared me. I did not want to continue life from just an existing standpoint. I had too much life, joy, and love in my heart for myself, my family, and the world. I had to dig deep to help mend my broken heart to some capacity that I would find and accept my new norm, move on with my life purpose, and rock the hell out of it. But first, I had to practice self-care at a 100 for a good while. Atlanta helped me process a little deeper of what I've been through and I experienced some sparks of joy whenever I could break away from the grief.

My family rallied around me and made sure I was okay every step of the way. I visited and spent time with six households of my family. I really love Atlanta and in the near future, I will spend more time there. One of my aunts in Atlanta, my Aunt Davine lost her husband 10 years prior and gave me wise counsel on steps to take toward my future. Thank you Auntie. Now on to a city with tons of primos that have sabor and fuego baby! Just what the doctor ordered...Orlando.

Orlando- I have a lot of family in the entire state of Florida, which amazes me when I think I can stop in almost every city from Jacksonville to Miami. Wow!

Orlando was the next place I felt I needed to visit and hangout with my family.

My sister came with me and it was such a beautiful time. Big fun just relaxing, watching Celia Cruz series on Netflix. Salsa dancing, good eats, exciting outings, and loud conversations always in Spanish, English and with a mix of Spanglish... gotta love it!

Every last one of my primos (cousins) are the bomb. One of my cousins is actually my second cousin, yet our family is very close so we sometimes forget that sometime, lost her beautiful husband the year before. I am forever grateful for the candid conversations we had about her experience. She was able to give me the special attention I needed at the right time to help lift my spirits up.
Gracias prima that was so needed. Loved this trip and it was so necessary in regaining my strength.

Los Millanes I love you all!!!!! This was my last trip away from Ohio before I prepared to leave our beautiful apartment that Renz and I loved so much. Now back home to regroup and pack some more.

Saying farewell to our wonderful space was hard yet necessary. I would not be able to move forward if I stayed there. I would have been frozen. I knew if I allowed myself to stay frozen, I would relinquish my power to persevere. I had to figure out a way, and push through the fear of the unknown without Renz, which was very hard.

Although five months had passed since his transition, I still felt like it was a bad dream and someone kind would wake me up from it. In my grief, I secretly waited for him to return. I felt like I was in a trapped bubble. I wanted a safe space that allowed me to think about my feelings in a free-flowing way without judgements from others. I really believed I could change this and get my happily ever after life back. I shared my deepest feelings with those that could understand the deep cut I was enduring. I also told my therapist everything from the depths of my soul. I never held back not even the strangest feelings that may not seem normal to the human mind. My intuition has always been very high since I was a child. I knew I had to rely on it even more. I knew I had to continue filling my cup. I could only hear from those that spoke life into me. Therefore, I surrounded myself with the right people from friends, family, soul sisters, mentors, and my life and business coaches. I immersed myself in their goodness and love. I created a toolbox of strong people around me and self-care tools I could reach for whenever I needed to.

Next up, I needed a road trip before surgery because I'd be sitting for a couple of months again. My next destination was a private trip I took with a mother and child that are very dear to me. We drove to Columbus, Ohio and had the best time. It was supposed to be an overnight trip turned full weekend trip where neither one of us wanted to return home. We enjoyed just being together at the hotel. We didn't need anything else. The truth is they were grieving as well and had a special space in their hearts for Lorenzo and I.

Having young children around while you're grieving is a beautiful thing, as they remind you of how full life is and how to embrace and seize every moment.

The biggest lesson I learned from this trip was to seize the moment. I left that trip on fire and ready for my surgery so I could get back to learning how to walk. I had too much work left for me to do on Earth. At this point, I had to learn how to grieve and take care of myself at the same time. A very tall order, indeed.

My second leg surgery was very successful and I worked extremely hard with my physical therapist to come back to life. I had the best physical therapist that believed in me and my purpose in life. She often told me she was inspired by me. It took another 90 days of hard work on crutches and gaining my strength in my body, mind and soul.

I love the team of family that rallied around me to make sure I got to and from therapy. Shoutout to my Titi Martha, my best friend sister Cynthia, and an incredible neighbor and friend Rotuaja. I was determined to learn how to walk and salsa dance by my 50th birthday party on November 22, 2019.

Testimonial by Ari Ledger, Shauna's Niece

The love my Tio had for my Titi was extraordinary! It was never one sided. They always came together as one, which made them so powerful and their love stronger.

Chapter 10

THE GREAT LOVE AFFAIR CONTINUES

I will be remiss if I didn't share with you some of the beautiful ways my husband has expressed his love to me while we are in two unique spaces. I feel his presence very strongly and think about him non-stop no matter what I do. I feel he is extremely proud of me making it happen. I feel like all of the counsel and advice he has given me over the years is not lost and that our LOVE is alive more now than ever. I am able to hear his advice and what he would tell me when I am making a decision. I decided to pick up where I left off with writing my children's books and the special projects I put a pause on until I felt well enough to get back to them.

In 2020, I went to London to participate in a business event hosted by my business coaches, Grace and Charlotte. The first time I went to London, I went with Lorenzo. We loved London! Therefore, I was happy to fly to London for a second time. The timing could not have been better. Special thanks to Nadine for allowing me to grieve and speak about my grief at will. I love you.

Nadine and I went to the Ice Bar in London. If you haven't been there, it is a must go. There are beautiful pieces of ice sculpture all around you. You are dressed in a cloak with attached gloves so you can handle your special drink in an ice block as your glass. Talk about numb lips lol. I was delighted that this was the same bar Lorenzo and I had been to years prior. However, Nadine added dinner to our ticket this time. We ate in the restaurant below the Ice Bar. It was a Chinese restaurant and it was Chinese New Year. Everyone in the restaurant received a golden egg passed out by the waitress. When you opened the golden egg there was a medal with an engraved message that was unique to each person.

My message was, "I will hold you in my heart until I hold you in heaven". All I could do was hold my head down and I was filled with emotions. I felt so connected with Lorenzo at that moment. She read my message silently and said out loud, "How appropriate."

Testimony by Mark A. Ledger, Shauna's Uncle

I could see when Lorenzo and Shauna were together at an early age that they were meant for each other, even if they could not see it. I remember when Shauna and Lorenzo were dating and they decided to go their separate ways that their love was meant for each other and each other only. When they were together and I would see them, it was like magic. The love was inseparable. I remember one time the two of them were spending time with my wife and I. We were out at a function and Lorenzo sat down at a piano pretending to play. Shauna drifted over, leaned against the piano, and pretended to sing as he played. It was like magic with the two of them. They were so much fun and the four of us just enjoyed ourselves. I will miss my nephew so much. He just had an aura about him.

Chapter 11

QUARANTINE 2020

F irst, we interrupt this story to tell you that it literally took me five months to get back to writing this chapter. I knew from the start that 11 was going to be the last chapter. The number 11 is significant to Lorenzo and I. His birthday is 4/11 and mine is 11/22. We thought it was so neat that we both shared the number 11 between us.

As I mentioned above, I had a major writer's gap and couldn't get this chapter completed on the timelines I thought I would. I ended up having to journal around this break in my writing. My inner mentor told me to journal about my feelings.

Through journaling, I discovered that somewhere in my grief mind, I told myself that the last chapter meant the love was over between Renz and I. I couldn't let that happen so I self-sabotaged my time. I did everything under the sun but to finish this story. Grief is a strange beast and you have to be very careful with it. Grief will take you down if you allow it to.

Anyone reading this chapter knows and understands completely what happened in the world in 2020. This year brought us all to a halt. We had to grieve the life we once knew, grieve loved ones that passed from Covid19, regroup, look in the mirror, get real with ourselves, and pick up the pieces with a new plan to learn how to live again. In a crazy sense, I felt like it was deja vu for me. My bereavement therapist asked me how do you feel about what's going on and what would Lorenzo have thought about this. I told her I felt like the world was hugging me right now. I felt like the world was experiencing my feelings from 2019-2020 with my first year of loss and grief. I felt compelled even more than ever to want to help the world figure out how to move from an old life to the new unknown life that lies ahead. I've been living through these tiers of life without the choice of stopping it or controlling it. I immediately was pushed into a space in which I had to:

- Let go.
- Trust the process.
- Know my worth.
- Continue the legacy.
- Work my purpose.
- Know my truth.

The year 2019-2020 was a major year of stretching and growing for me. I'm a different person now. I even look different when I look in the mirror. My spirit is different. It is a good thing in a way because I am re-learning about me and my purpose. I need a different outlook on life so that I can achieve my life's purpose which is my number one agenda from here on out.

I'll grieve for Lorenzo my entire life. I've given myself permission to stay in the present and hold on to joy all at the same time. We all process loss and traumatic experiences differently. Do whatever you have to get yourself back to a healthy space. It's worth it. We only have one life to live and we have to live it to the fullest. I promised myself that I would. One of the things my husband would never like is for me to give up on life. I never wanted to disappoint him or myself.

This endless love thing he and I got going on is precious and I know this special kind of love that I've experienced will be with me throughout my lifetime. I am so honored to be his chosen wife. Honored for the lifetime we spent together. I'm an empowered woman that is driven and will continue our legacy and my personal life's purpose at this time. All of the people I've mentioned above and experiences I had with them are the only way I could figure out how to get to the point of wanting to live again. As I'm writing this, Lorenzo passed a little over a year and a half ago. For me, this all seems to have happened yesterday. I'm in a very strong space working on myself to find myself. My new self that has been forever changed because I have a love affair that is endless. This is the most beautiful gift of it all. My love will never end and I will never forget what I meant to him. I hope and pray that anyone reading this story has or will embark on a love that sustains you forever and ever.

I have no clue what lies tomorrow, yet I made a promise to myself to stay in the present, focus on what I can control, and continue to pour goodness in my life everyday. I am committed to staying humble, being focused on my journey, meditating, and taking care of my mind, body and soul.

Lastly, I promise to surround myself with genuine, loving people. My message to everyone reading this book is that I hope that you are rejuvenated and ready to continue life with love, joy, and inspiration just as I am. I wish you all much love and success with your relationships and pray you have an opportunity to meet your soul mate in this lifetime. As tears run down my face right now, I know that it is not the end. I hope this love story inspires you to believe in the meaning of true love and that it starts with loving yourself.

Much peace and love,

Shauna

S hauna Hibbitts an author, transformational coach, motivational speaker, podcast host, facilitator, and early childhood specialist with over 30 years of experience that engages her audience in both English and Spanish. While she loves to travel and has called many places home, Shauna is a proud Cleveland, Ohio native and remains appreciative of her days growing up in a sports town near the Lake Erie area. She is a proud board member for Frontline Services and a Toastmaster member of Cleveland.

Photo by: Jeanette Brewster
All original chapter photos retouched by JEAN B. & CO.
(jeanettebrewster.com)

Printed in the USA
CPSIA information can be obtained
at www.ICGtesting.com
LVHW051437180224
772154LV00009B/104